THE VISIBLE CHURCH

THE VISIBLE CHURCH

Dennis C. Benson

ABINGDON PRESS
NASHVILLE

THE VISIBLE CHURCH

Copyright © 1988 Dennis C. Benson

This book is printed on acid-free paper.

BENSON, DENNIS C.

The visible church / Dennis C. Benson.
p.   cm.
ISBN 0-687-43770-9 (pbk.: alk. paper)
1. Mass media in religion.   I. Title.
BV652.95.B46   1988   88-21930
254.3—dc19   CIP

MANUFACTURED BY THE PARTHENON PRESS AT
NASHVILLE, TENNESSEE, UNITED STATES OF AMERICA

To Ruth Rylander—

creative spirit,
woman of faith
—and friend

CONTENTS

PREFACE

It would be a morning to remember. Mother and young son had just returned from shopping. The small boy toddled into the apartment with his mother. She placed a bag of groceries on the kitchen table and dropped her keys on the counter.

When she went back outside to pick up a second bag, the unthinkable happened. A gust of wind caught the door and it slammed shut. Mother and child were suddenly on opposite sides of a locked door.

The small child instantly realized that he was separated from his mother. He became hysterical. The desperate mother could feel her rising panic in the screams of her frightened son. She shouted to the people in neighboring apartments for help. What could she do to comfort her infant?

My mother coaxed me to push my small fingers under the door. She put her hand over mine, and as she stroked my fingers, I could feel her love and caring during those moments of separation. My sobbing was reduced to sniffles, and we waited, fingers touching, until the building superintendent came to rescue me.

VISIBLE AND INVISIBLE

There always have been believers who longed to feel God's presence, to see God and feel God's touch. The visible manifestation of the eternal and invisible reality of life is difficult to sustain apart from our experience of faith. God's love, expressed in the act of incarnation through Jesus Christ, acknowledges this human need. Jesus understood Thomas' need to touch, to see that the resurrection was a reality.

An invisible church has been founded by God and sustained by the work and power of the Holy Spirit. And this reality is reflected in all our organizations, plans, and work. In moments of stress, failure, and pain, it is this invisible church, our spiritual mother, that touches the visible church with love and compassion.

Cast of Thousands

In these pages you will meet the models of ministry offered by creative brothers and sisters from around the world. I will name many of them; many more will slip by without notice.

People in the church and professional media worlds have taught me. Charles Brackbill, Dick Gilbert, Bob Thompson, Dick Crew, Derek Simons, Ron Byler, Jerry Lackamp, Ed Willingham, Hal Dragseth, Carolyn Manlove, Ben Gums, Bill Huie, Bob Schutt, Gregg Hartung, John Ciampa, Bob Harper, Jimmy Roach, Linda Carducci, Tom Boomershine, and countless others have been my companions as teachers and students in the world of media.

I have also been assisted indirectly by my students at United Theological Seminary: Douglas Alder, Silke and Joachim H. Hartner, David Hiatt, Bradford Olson, Jerry Hemrich, Jane Strippel, Carmen Wooster, Cheryl Witmer, Mike Anderson, Jon and Lynn Clark.

Most of the stories and practical ideas come from ordinary folks who have been driven by God to do the extraordinary. Often they have used the barest of resources to touch the lives of thousands. These folks who share their quest to embrace the world with the Good News have seldom taken a communications course, nor have they had a background in television or advertising. Yet, they all have drawn upon the oldest and most traditional resource of the Christian church: the beckoning of the Holy Spirit.

Dangerous

This is a deliciously dangerous book. It beckons you into the scary realm of what can be done. Or perhaps even more frightening, what you can make happen. You will encounter some of the most inspired and practical opportunities for authentic ministry.

You will witness testimonies to the possibility that now, at this moment, you can find new wineskins for the eternal gospel of Christ for your setting. How does your current ministry look, compared to what the visible church can be?

This book can make you restless with what you have done or not done in the past. The testimonies of others will confront you with your responsibility to see that ways to present the gospel deserve the same excitement and vitality as is offered by the content of that gospel.

On the other hand, the blueprints, hunches, and visions in these pages can seduce you into focusing on forms and techniques of communication, rather than the content of ministry. There is something very wonderful about mastering an electronic medium. It gives the practitioner an amazing sense of power and satisfaction. So it is important to remember that there is no *one* answer to all our daily problems in the parish.

"Let's produce a video."

John Ciampa, my colleague in video production, and I seem to be faced with this demand at every meeting with clients. Video may or may not be the answer for a particular client. The appropriate medium must be based on the message and the receivers. Every means of communicating the saving message of Jesus Christ is merely a way to make this reality accessible to others.

It is our prayer that God will give you spectacles of faith through which you can see the visible church. Such a community of possibility, hope, and justice in Jesus Christ must be shared with a dying world. Besides, it is fun to live dangerously.

Dennis C. Benson
United Theological Seminary
Dayton, Ohio

Chapter 1

THE INVISIBLE CHURCH

"So we have *agape, eros,* and *philos.*" The student finished his lengthy oral summary of Swedish Bishop Nygren's famous exposition on the New Testament's use of the three Greek words for *love*. Joseph Haroutunian, our systematic theologian, paused in his pacing of the classroom aisle. "We could call that concept . . . Swedish love."

We roared in laughter. The quip made its point. Haroutunian had been concerned for months with our unfortunate tendency to "humpty-dumpty" our words. As first-year students in theology, we tended to give "faith words" any subjective meaning we wanted, regardless of context.

The term *media* is often stroked, massaged, and twisted to achieve any context and meaning desired. The adjectives *electronic, parabolic,* or *digital* tend to confuse us. *Media* has come to mean everything—and nothing. We need a much more simple and basic understanding of this popular label for these new devices that change and challenge us in such a revolutionary manner.

For the sake of this book, the plural *media* is used to describe the means by which information, values, or emotions are transmitted, translated, or transferred to another person. Such a definition includes physical, aural, graphic, electric, and other methods of communication. Perhaps we still will need to humpty-dumpty our definition as we move through this complex world.

Every age is really a media age. The dominant forms of communication have shifted and changed. Each of the ingredients that sustains a culture influences all the other

13

ingredients. Yet our age is different from past ages. A new set of
factors has shifted benchmark values, life-styles, and personal
context. We will touch on this more in the chapters that follow.

It is an escalating and exasperating journey for the person of
faith who ministers in this age. Modern Sirens wail to seduce
those who contribute to the building of the visible church. They
beckon the media person to crash upon the rocks of elitism.
Therefore, it is imperative that we who seek to give flesh to the
body of faith have clear starting points, and the invisible church
provides our bearings for the trek.

Our journey into the contemporary witness of the visible
church is based on the reality of the invisible church, a spiritual
community of faith which cuts across all time, communication
forms, and trials. It is this foundation upon which the visible
church of our day must take form. This foundation can be
reflected only through a mirror darkly as we work to shape an
authentic contemporary visible expression. Yet it is our
relationship with the source of the invisible church which leads
us boldly into the present and future.

THE SOURCE OF THE INVISIBLE CHURCH

The Creator God is the source of our message, shape, and
form. The content of the proclamation is the God who created us,
sustains us, redeems us, and beckons us to share what has
happened to us. Yet, the bonding between creator and creature
is so intimate that it is hard to examine it apart from our own lives
and work. This means that the communicator, or initiator, of the
means for sharing the Word must always be aware of who and
whose he or she is. This is not always easy, for the practical
process of finding communication flesh for the experience of the
Creator often overwhelms the bonding between God and
creation itself.

Therefore the occasion of duplicating this relationship to
communicate the faith must focus on the sovereignty, majesty,
love, and justice of God. For instance, the many examples of
touching the needs of the world which we share in this book are
not motivated by humanism. We are, rather, seeking to maintain
the relationship with the Creator that was established through

the act of creation ("and God saw that it was good"). We must care for all of God's creation. Restoration, redemption, and resurrection form the content of our message. Yet we seek models to make a visible expression of that which is above, beyond, and within the contemporary faith community.

Jesus Christ is the medium and the message for all those who are seeking ways to bring the gospel to others. God became flesh so that we might experience the reality of God's love. The Incarnation is the ultimate example of our understanding of "media."

This means that the most profound and most authentic media for communicating the gospel are our very lives. Each person becomes a medium for the message of Christ! Indeed, the electronic media can be viewed as merely an extension of our bodies. The human senses and sensibilities have been cloned and broadly communicated through the public media forms. This electronic and digital mimicry is crude in comparison to human beings, but the technical clones of human resources and needs carry great power.

These generalized comments about God the creator as the content of our message is most fully made known to us, personally and particularly, in the birth, life, death, and resurrection of Jesus. The meaning of creation, forgiveness, love, justice, and discipleship is made most abundantly clear in the biblical witness to Jesus Christ.

The implications for those who venture into the intentional manifestation of the Incarnation in their lives are extremely demanding and rewarding. If you bear the name of Jesus Christ so that others can experience him in you, the forces of the world are likely to respond to you as they did to him. If you reach out to offer the hospitality of Christ to the lost, confused, and uncomely, through the forms of public electronic communication, there will be controversy, resistance, and persecution. The cross remains the standard for this model in our quest to bring media and ministry together.

The promise upon which we can base our task is that God will not abandon us. Jesus Christ will bless you with a richness of life and ministry beyond anything you have ever imagined. You will feel the surging skin-close bonding between Christ and your efforts and dreams. The quest to undertake the challenge of this book is an act of faith and faithfulness. God will bless you as you seek media opportunities to share the gospel with others. But the energy to overcome the resistance within us and around us to be the offshoots of our faith roots is not based simply on good intentions or optimism.

The leadership of the Creator God and the model of Christ, the servant brother, are pieces of our faith to which every Christian looks for guidance. Yet it is often the pounding encounter between these spiritual resources and the practicality of our daily ministries which grinds away our resolve. The reading of the Bible, books about church growth, and practical manuals on publicity for the local congregation is proper and fitting. Yet you and I know how hard it is to move from good ideas, or even inspiring moments, to reality.

"How do I find the time to do something like that?"

"You don't know how conservative my people are."

"We are a small church with no resources. How can we hope to use media?"

Such honest probes confront me at every workshop. In fact, I face the same questions myself when I am about to undertake a new communication challenge. George Lucas, who fathered a revolution in popular films with his *Star Wars* trilogy, was asked about his feelings concerning his first big success. "*Star Wars* represented 40 percent of what I set out to accomplish. I ran out of time and money."

We are called to risk boldly for the sake of the gospel. God forgives those who risk and fail. We are called to be faithful to the content of the faith, not successful in terms of the evaluation of others.

The Holy Spirit is the source of energy which makes this high calling of communicating the gospel a possibility. There are many ways in which the Christian church deals with this aspect of God's relationship with us. It is my understanding that the Holy Spirit is the contemporary presence of God in our lives. The comforter, counselor, or advocate is the very power which enables us to move from thought to action on behalf of the ministry of Jesus Christ.

The Holy Spirit is given to the community of faith. It is not a solo gift provided for individuals. The tough imperatives in the book of Acts calling us to "rise up" compel those whom God beckons to give themselves in servanthood to the community. Christians in the early church were not permitted to bask in the glow of revelation on the Damascus Road or at the day of Pentecost. They were compelled to rise up and share the manifestation of the Holy Spirit with the whole creation.

On the other hand, the Holy Spirit creates our personhood by which each of us is unique and particular. We are formed and sustained as persons before God. While an individual may need only a rifle and a horse to survive on a frontier wilderness, or a hot car and a VCR in a community of condos, a person finds meaning and reality only in the context of community. We need to acknowledge and practice being a part of the whole body of Christ in order to celebrate the gift of the Holy Spirit.

There are times when the visible church is absent. At least, it may seem that we are alone in that hospital room as the doctor prepares to bring us bad news. Indeed, the moment of preaching or teaching is lonely when things aren't going well. Yet the Holy Spirit places us in the context of the communion of saints, which is both visible and invisible. The Spirit weds us to those who have lived, are living, and are yet to live in Christ.

It is a lonely moment when we stand before a governing board to present a radically new plan for evangelism, stewardship, ministry, or fellowship—a plan that utilizes fresh media forms. Yet, we are not there alone. Abraham, Sarah, Peter, St. Francis, Wesley, and Nelson Mandela are there with us through the activity of the Holy Spirit! When we pray, the whole church—past, present, and future—gathers with us.

The work of the Holy Spirit through the communion of saints helps us also in more practical ways. For instance, when we must struggle to put together a new plan to bring more people into a dying Sunday school, we are not facing a hopeless task. The whole church of Jesus Christ is present through the Holy Spirit. Ideas from others become ours to utilize, change, and transform. Every vision is possible under the power of the Holy Spirit.

The Holy Spirit performs in the realm which mass media has so successfully tapped. It is the Spirit that arouses, entertains, comforts, gathers, amuses, and challenges. The electronic web that surrounds us has been extremely adept at snaring the media consumer through these areas of human need. How do the Spirit and the electronic extensions of our senses touch? How do they differ? What are the realms of Christian witness yet to be probed in the electronic environment?

The Holy Spirit is also the source of our comfort and support as media producers and enablers. Many of our ventures on behalf of the gospel will meet with criticism, contention, and crisis. No one can faithfully navigate the journey into the world of media without support. The dangers of distraction, discouragement, and seductive delight await each person of faith. Yet the Holy Spirit truly makes all things possible through Jesus Christ.

A heady realistic optimism undergirds those who are fueled by the Holy Spirit. This book celebrates possibilities from those who have experienced the harsh reality of carrying the faith into very unfriendly environments.

The Holy Spirit forces us to address the pessimism that is so popular among many in the national, regional, and local ministry. It has been particularly easy for those caught in the leadership tension between hope and despair to blame the church's failure to extend the gospel to people in the world on the theological differences in the mainline churches. "They are always challenging my theology when I suggest that we reach out through newspaper ads."

However, the role of the Holy Spirit quickly dispels this excuse for failure. God, working through the Holy Spirit, communicates a unity to the body of Christ that is deeper than human opinions. The witness of history reveals that the sinful creature has always created splits within the body. Our insecurity, sinful pride, and denial of God's freedom to speak to anyone have resulted in a paralyzing practice of judging others. It is God alone who judges us concerning our faithfulness. The opinions of contemporaries simply do not have final authority.

In fact, I have found that the people who differ from me theologically often have become my best supporters. The older, more conservative believers have upheld me and my work most faithfully. When people are grounded in Christ, fueled by the Holy Spirit, understand and accept you, those people will always give you a chance to be faithful to your vision.

I remember telling the folks in a little church I served that I would be going to Selma to join Dr. King and his group. The dear folks in that church shook their heads. "We don't agree with you.

Yet, we know you are not a communist. You feel that Christ is
guiding you to be with those people."

I went. They understood—and continued to disagree. The
specific dreams and plans in this book provide possibilities for
every community! If your people love Jesus Christ, you simply
have no grounds for blaming your congregation because there is
no outreach through media.

There is a frightening implication to such an affirmation of the
Holy Spirit's role in the stance of an embracing congregation.
Could it be that the congregation that does not support a more
visible church does not know Jesus Christ and is not responsive
to the Holy Spirit? Such a fear cannot be an excuse for leaders
who seek to nudge their church into faithfulness. At every
moment in history the local congregation is forced to look
carefully at its basic commitment to Jesus Christ. This is the role
of lay and clergy ministry leadership.

THE VISIBLE CHURCH

My colleague in video production, John Ciampa, and I visited
seven of the fastest growing churches in a major denomination.
We were struck by three insights.

First, each church demonstrated an intentional visibility as a
caring church in the community. Each one took the faith to the
streets. For instance, a church in Puerto Rico was filled with
nicely dressed men, women, and children. Into the midst of this
comfortable congregation came a retarded street person. He
couldn't talk and was dirty from sleeping, as one member
described it, "wherever the night met him." Yet he embraced
me and obviously was an accepted part of the congregation. He
could feel Christ being communicated through the medium of
these people's lives.

Second, we were stunned by the power role played by the laity
in the leadership of those churches. At one church we shot video
for ten hours. The minister talked to us for fifteen minutes and
we didn't see him again. Lay people led us through all the many
mission projects, church groups, and activities. It was *their*
ministry that was being shared.

Third, John and I were impressed by the role of the clergy in
enabling all this to happen. The clergy in those seven churches

represented every possible style. Some were stunning preachers, others were dull, but they all seemed to be rooted in their
understanding that it is the body of Christ that provides the spark
for renewal and outreach.

The Holy Spirit also communicates and confirms a sense of
history to those who risk for the gospel. The Spirit helps us
remember that we are part of a kinship that goes back four
thousand years, to the mothers and fathers of the tribe. The
contemporary church seems to have denied this great gift.
People often act under the influence of nostalgia—the way we
wish things had been:

"Remember how the last pastor had such short homilies?"

"Wasn't it nice when we had a minister who chose only gospel
hymns?"

"Remember when the Sunday school was filled because we
taught the true faith?"

Nostalgia destroys all hope for the present and the future. This
foggy sense of what happened keeps changing the past to make
today seem terrible. The reality of history communicates the way
things really were, and the message of that truth is startling. Our
fathers and mothers in the faith remained faithful in the face of
the most unbelievable trials and difficulties. They risked to
provide education for the poor through the Sunday school. They
preached against slavery when that attitude was not popular.
They were hung on meat hooks, died in gas chambers, and were
beaten on the streets for taking their witness to the world.
History frees us! If our forebears in the faith utilized risky ways of
bringing Christ to others, then we can do it in our day! True
creativity is based on an appreciation of history. God is the God
who acts in history.

AND SO . . .

The church is the most creative institution on earth! We are
sitting on a volcano of power. The world is crying out for the
message of the gospel. The competitive gospels of our society
have failed. Yet a growing number of people continue to wander
outside the loving embrace of God.

Therefore, the church is challenged to make visible whose she
is. She is called by Creator, Jesus the Christ, and the Holy Spirit

to put on her true flesh, so that others might know the gospel. The way of the cross is not easy. Pain on this path is to be expected. Faithfulness to the gospel is costly. Yet it is possible to make the love of God in Jesus Christ visible through the church.

For those wandering into this media maze, it is challenging to be a leader in a local church. If you shared my theological training, you never had a communication or media course. You focused on the traditional theological disciplines: biblical languages, church history, and pastoral care. You also drew upon the teaching and preaching models of your mentors. Yet a new age is upon us. The gap between the visible message of the world and our public proclamation of the faith is widening by the moment.

The clergy and lay leaders of the church are being offered a foundation for personal reformation, resurrection, or reconfirmation. God is calling you at this moment to be that which God has made you to be in Jesus Christ. This is absolutely the best time to be alive in ministry!

The church is the most supportive institution on earth. If people don't support you in a new ministry venture, there are two possible reasons. They either don't understand what you are talking about, or it is a bad idea! If you have an idea inspired by God, and your folks understand it, they will always support you! It is a great time to lead the church into the quest for finding the communication flesh of the gospel.

- Never has the world so longed for the saving work of Jesus Christ.
- Never has there been a more relevant body of theology and history to support us as a foundation for faithfulness in the world.
- Never has there been such a host of witnesses from the past, present, and future.
- Never have there been so many resources and opportunities to make visible the Good News.

Thank God we are alive at this moment, with this calling, for these people!

Chapter 2

THE VISIBLE WORLD

"When you see people carrying rifles and shooting in the streets, the revolution hasn't arrived. It has actually been here for five years. The street riots are merely visible signs of a past reality." These comments touch upon all of us at this time in history. The worries of network executives over lost audiences, parents' concern over youths held hostage by video cassettes— these indicate a change that "has actually been here for years." A communication revolution is completed; the fallout has only now become apparent. Each day it is more apparent that the connectional linear past is gone, and the invisible erratic communication future has come.

The aggressive spread of communication modes beyond our control and understanding has upset the way each of us thinks, dreams, acts, believes, prays, and loves. And, this virus-like revolution also infects and disables our formal and informal institutions. People feel that suddenly everything is out of focus. They are not able to clearly identify any connection between past, present, and future values and needs.

Those who believed in material security have seen the visible affirmation of such belief swept away. New economic modes have shattered traditional industrial, financial, and labor structures. Pain, confusion, and conflict grip many caught in this social spasm.

Those who focused on sensuality have seen this source of visible delight brutally shaken. Cancer, AIDS, and hundreds of other diseases that ravage the flesh and mind are daily media realities.

Those who believe in the redemptive power of politics or the democratic process have been robbed of their linear promises as they encounter the complexity of the media maze. Battered innocents, assassinated leaders, economic failure, censored media, inhuman prisons, and rights-denied minorities have taken the edge off utopian political systems. The cameras, the microphones—the unblinking eye of the international media web has exposed the failure of human progress to ensure justice and equality. Technological miracles do not ensure a better life.

Those who believe in an insular ethnocentric worldview have seen the media pierce the walls of race, nationality, class, and religion. On the news, the haunting eyes of a starving African child penetrate our hearts during our evening meal.

A man, a woman, and two children huddle together and stare directly at us. With tears, the mother shares the pain caused by the closing of the mill or the lost family farm.

A fourteen-year-old girl struggles to hold a pose of defiance on the 42nd Street corner. The runaway tries to be tough. Her lip quivers as a car slides to the curb and the man asks her how much she charges for her services. Fathers and mothers across the country experience the possibility that this girl could be their daughter.

A black grandmother bravely cares for her dying grandchild who is suffering from AIDS. She has no money and no support. Yet she will not give up the doomed child. Every white, red, and brown parent across the world can relate to her pain and courage.

The visible world is no longer visible in the same way it has been in the past. Communication now provides the key to power, control, and understanding. Yet several factors make such a taming of the media maze difficult.

OVERLOAD: TOO MUCH IS NOT ENOUGH

"I have seen the media experiences produced by Harvey Cox and Sister Corita back in the 1960s, but what you did last night is something very different. You were showing us what happens in our minds as we face the overload of too many messages and sensual stimuli." A noted biblical scholar was commenting on my presentation of the previous evening. I had bathed the audience in an aural and visual experience created by a stereo sound track and six images from four slide projectors and two movie projectors.

He had captured my very point! How do we sort out the linear, or step-by-step, logic and ordering of our lives in the face of too much from too many different directions? The mental and emotional sorting process upon which we were raised in the premedia period is no longer very helpful. There are simply too many messages offered in too many different ways. It sometimes seems as if TILT has flashed across our cognitive center. What does it all mean?

I remember the days of my early multimedia productions. I would carefully construct the presentations around a linear sound track. But when I flooded the audience with the mix of several simultaneous media stimuli they were overwhelmed.

"It doesn't make any sense."

"It was just a lot of confusion."

"It was so violent."

"Why can't things be simple again?"

These comments reflect the kind of chaos the media mix seems to inflict on those who come from the linear, or more step-by-step organization, era. Yet, all of us are changing or have been changed by the media. We become a part of what we experience. It is a virus, good and bad, which locks into our system.

On the other hand, retired people who were educated with a McGuffey *Reader* in a one-room schoolhouse are now some of the most sophisticated media buffs. After watching one hundred television commercials a day, they have experienced the latest in visual and aural techniques.

The media overload changes many things about the people who are engaged in the visible media world. The internal pacing and spacing of input or learning patterns are transformed. It is as if a phone system has been rewired or a computer has been reprogrammed. People who feast on video, audio, and digital media find that their appetites change radically. The electronic fast-food diet of the media maze makes it very hard to digest the slower, less sensually demanding content of the past.

Such media conditioning makes the church, school, and other important institutions seem remote and inaccessible to our imagination and loyalty. The media-massaged consumer finds that the traditional sermon or political lecture easily induces drowsiness or boredom. Even the oldest linear-oriented elders of the tribe nod off during worship.

VIDEO KIDS

The children of the video revolution also are affected in strange ways by the visible world. It is often assumed that the young easily slide into this strange world of intermixed stimuli, messages, and demands. But human culture does not march on through revolutions in a clean, carefully bordered progression. We all have experienced the emotional "nag" between generations, triggered by the culture lag in a time of acknowledged change. Yet both young and old are battered by the perception whirlwind that separates the past and the present.

Siblings often have a difficult time understanding each other because of the careful media marketing channeling each has experienced. The media models of an eleven-year-old female differ radically from those of her thirteen-year-old sister. And both will throw away the media forms, with their stars and artifacts, as they move on to the next market niche.

Where are the viable human models for growth? In my experience, young people don't really want to be like the one-dimensional personages who march across the music videos. They may be attracted to the attributes that are fed into the image in quest of a market, but no one would really want to be such a person.

Grandparents no longer live across the street. There was a time when young people could run away to grandmother's house. The elders of the tribe aren't easily available for long talks over cookies and milk. Parents and other significant adults are programmed by society (and by the church) to be together as little as possible. Intergenerational programming still has not won much acceptance in most churches.

Young and old in the same household often have little experience with each other. How do young people discover, test, and embrace moral and ethical patterns for themselves when there are no viable guidelines? The standards of the past are faded and jaded by the media maze until they seem irrelevant. Even the easy salad-bar ethics of the day seem unappealing and meaningless. As Mick Jagger suggests in the MTV commercial, "Too much is not enough."

NEW WINE, OLD WINESKINS

"I can do anything a mule can do." The man stood before my dad's desk, offering his most convincing appeal in his quest for employment. Unfortunately, there are too many mules in a world that requires artists.

It is ironic that often, even those who produce the content and form of modern media are locked into a world of linear requirements. A written script, an organizational structure which requires a line of command for decisions, a pandering view of the audience, and a profit-oriented system tie the hands of one who could capture the unfolding reality by just pointing a camera and bringing the story to the world.

The secular wineskins in which mass media are shaped and distributed are also caught between two ages. The keepers of the spring are as restricted as those who feel the burden.

People of faith who feel the damaging edge of this new media world are often angry and vindictive toward media people. These righteous people act as if the media's presentations of distortion or ugliness really are the problem. But counting the gunshots, bare thighs, or dirty words in a television show or rock song does not contribute to the resolution of the problem. These unwelcome moments are just symptoms of the revolution itself.

It is true that individuals contribute to the aspects of a film or a song. However, they must work within a web of expectation and demand which makes them mere links in a wider process.

The gospel places upon us the responsibility of dealing with good and evil in the visible world. Adam and Eve couldn't get away with blaming the snake. It is really a disservice to place all the blame for the abuses of modern communication on the media.

Christians in community also are responsible for what they do with each moment of choice. When parents focus solely on rock stars as the source of youth's problems, they are failing their children. Consumers are responsible for what they do with what is presented in media. Good and evil will always be before us.

Yet, how do we make decisions about what oozes into our most intimate life moments in elevators, public restrooms, dentists' offices, and headsets?

The economic system that controls mass media makes special demands on those who produce the mass-media world. There is a link between the audience and the systems that bring us music and messages. It doesn't make much difference whether a system is publicly supported or commercials pay the freight. The audience must be pleased in order for the messages to be distributed. If the customer doesn't like the media product, he or she will turn it off (and displease advertisers) or not buy the product (and displease advertisers). This means that communication systems focus on pleasing the lowest common denominator in their audiences.

It is certainly a low aesthetic standard to base your media art on the desires of the audience. Although this is one basic principle of all mass media, there are people and moments in which such a cynical view is not always in control. George Lucas (*Star Wars*) and Steven Spielberg (*E.T.*) have shown us that occasionally media artists can reach inside themselves for stories that touch the best in everyone.

HOPE FOR THE CHURCH FROM THE VISIBLE WORLD

"At every commercial break, get down on the floor and do sit-ups until the program resumes." My karate instructor may have been challenging me to get into better shape, but he was only partially kidding. His suggestion may be a radical act, but there are ways in which mass media can be recycled.

It is easy to be swept away with media criticism. Much can be shared about the dangers, failures, and difficulties in the web of media around us. Yet the redemptive power of the gospel conveys to us the possibility of transformation. There is nothing that cannot be recycled into a means of glorifying God. In fact, the awareness of the media revolution can provide the community of faith with an extraordinary opportunity.

"Haven't the recent scandals hurt your work in religious radio and television?" The woman was asking an honest question. However, the inquiry does hint that because some have abused the electronic media in the name of faith, it might not be used for good by others. It is my contention that the saving message of Jesus Christ can be presented through the stories of people who have been changed by God. The mass media provides one of the freshest moments in all history for presenting the gospel.

AND SO . . .

Many clues for ministry exist in this media maze. As I have suggested, the Holy Spirit can change the fragmentation of contemporary change into a moment of wholeness. It is my hunch that the experiential probes of electronic media can work on the same parts of our lives that receive the work of the Holy Spirit. This explains why people are so deeply touched and altered by electronic media experiences.

What would happen if we could bring media opportunities into the service of the gospel? I am suggesting more than simply placing a camera in a worship service. Doesn't the confusion of a world with disposable history long for continuity? How is the God of history revealed in a nonlinear setting? How does the communion of saints, the invisible church, relate to the collective community or to the tribal drum of modern media? How can the new wineskin of mass media become the vessel for the new wine?

These questions must be addressed in the theological discussions of the future. No one is really in charge of the media maze. It is a pulsating burst of power running wild in our lives. Hasn't God given us dominion over all creation? How do we keep the potential of God's media gift in the midst of so much criticism?

Chapter 3

THE VISIBLE CHURCH IN
THE VISIBLE WORLD

"I never watch television myself." A religious leader thought he was impressing us with his high principles.

Someone else brought him back to earth: "Well, each night I go home and watch television while I cook my hamburger. It brings me comfort and stimulates my own media work." He was striking back at the elitism which controls too many religious experts on mass media.

People who speak for the mainline churches on media matters often assume that they alone can judge television and radio. They seem to say that the public cannot possibly discern values for itself. Frequently these good folks have seen their own attempts to work with mass media dissolve. One can understand a certain bitterness when, so far, mainline Christianity's witness to Christ through mass media has struggled without success.

One of the most obvious criticisms that disables the church's outreach through modern media is the thesis that electronic communication is bad. These folks assemble impressive arguments about the impact of this new means of communication on traditional life. The family doesn't gather before the fire and read the Bible every night, as it did at one time.

These scenarios contrast the "good old days" to a sterile presentation of our present day of individual televisions, personal phones in each room, and a loss of family life. There is truth in such analysis. Marshal McLuhan, the late guru of media awareness, helped us realize that the medium of communication is as important as the content of the message. Something read alone is different from the personal storytelling of your mother.

McLuhan also teaches that we must put our insights within historical contexts. It is easy to have a "rear-view mirror" perspective on the unfolding future. Contemporary analysis of values is very dangerous when our standards for good and bad are based on a nostalgic view of the past.

Many facets of contemporary life are distressing. The family, marriage, and child care are facing very real challenges. But these aspects of life have always been threatened. There never has been a safe time or a best time for marriage and children—at any time in history. And we can judge history only within a particular historical context.

The disciplines of history and communication have great difficulty relating to each other. Each field has had trouble finding a place to stand so that it may apply its perspective to the other. The nature of modern media is its disposable quality, while history is built upon selective retrieval of information bits. And the number of bits is increasing at an amazing rate. For example, one might still find one or two inventory slips from farm families in western Pennsylvania in the 1770s. Now we can review every water bill—for the past fifty years—for the million people who live in the same region!

When we speak of modern media, either as critics or as contributors to the field, we must fight our romantic impulses. Most consistent theological critics of modern communication are romantic about the way the world should be or was. They add a great deal through their prophetic zeal. However, they should not immobilize the church from seeking a faithful ministry of transformation.

On the other hand, those who look at modern media in a constructive manner also may be carried away with the promises of technology. The present electronic revolution, in itself, offers no more or less possibility for serving the Kingdom than the dominant media of other ages. We will not be saved by the media world. It is Christ, working through us, who makes faithfulness possible at every moment, through every means.

THE BABY AND THE BATH WATER

Most books on religious media focus on the dangers and failures of media materials. Their particular examples of abuse do

indicate failure and evil. Yet, it is interesting to note that each
wave of media change has evoked violent reaction from those
who are products of the previous dominant medium.

Protests to the change in communication mode often are
registered by those with investments in the previous dominant
medium. For instance, when the once-dominant oral medium
was replaced by print, critics pointed to the wars, social
displacement, and religious revolution that followed as a result.
There are reasons to worry about the presence of the visible
electronic media that surrounds us with its incredible power.
Indeed, specific examples of programming do shock and abuse
our sensitivities. However, there is a newborn babe in that dirty
bath water.

As John Ciampa likes to remind me, there have been poor and
abusive expressions in communication forms of every age. Not
every playwright in the Elizabethan era wrote as well as
Shakespeare. In fact, most plays, books, operas, films, sermons,
or message of any age are much less than classic. The limited
classic best of the past is saved while the majority of poor quality
is lost. Therefore, it is to be expected that the greatest
communication explosion in history will produce the greatest
amount of poor art.

In light of the difficulty of presenting media material of
life-giving quality, I am amazed that so much fine media work
does exist in our day. There is great television. In fact, each week
on commercial networks, one can find ten or more hours of video
programming which affirm the human spirit, entertain the
imagination, and challenge the vision.

In spite of the panels that remind us about dirty words in pop
songs, many great songs are written and heard. You can find
much music that is uplifting and inspiring. The video cassette
offerings are amazing! Outstanding films keep popping up at the
local theater.

Given all the economic, cultural, and social limitations of
media systems, it is encouraging that brilliant examples of
life-giving media material can be found. The redemptive power
of the gospel does convey to us the possibility and responsibility
of transformation, for even the most despicable media forms.
There is nothing that cannot be recycled into a means of
glorifying God. In fact, the awareness of the media revolution

can provide the community of faith with an extraordinary opportunity.

"I think this situation proves that Christianity cannot be presented on television." A famed theologian was quite satisfied in his televised conclusions concerning recent scandals and misuse of the medium by television evangelists. I disagree.

Because some folks tried to be the church and stumbled into human sin, it does not mean that others in the community of Christ cannot be faithful through mass media opportunities. We stand with the apostle Paul on the threshold of a whole new world. As he sometimes failed in his ministry, so will we in our world. Jesus Christ simply calls us to the moment and media at hand for proclamation of the gospel.

GOLDEN ARCHES AND MORE

"It is hard to explain to my peers at seminary what I am doing in your course." The student was sharing her discomfort with some of the assignments I had given. She and her classmates had been sent out on weekly research expeditions to some of the most unlikely places of study. They visited fast-food restaurants, banking institutions, medical services, shopping malls, car dealerships, grocery stores, clothing stores, and beauty parlors/ barbershops.

"We can't present the gospel like McDonald's sells hamburgers." This assumption is right. However, my students went out with the perspective of the apostle Paul as he ventured into the alien Greco-Roman world. He searched for means by which the gospel could transform language, images, events, and persons into occasions for presenting the Cross of Christ.

It was amazing what my students found on their weekly forays. They observed, participated, and explored to discover what each of those visible forms was intentionally or unintentionally communicating to those who received their messages and services. These insights were compared to those gathered from the visible churches they attended each week.

"At McDonald's you received a clear message from its very appearance of what you could expect inside. The entrances were well marked, the floors clean, and the decorations bright and pleasant. The bathrooms were accessible for those with handicaps. If you spilled something, a person was there immediately with apologies for *your* accident!"

"When I compared the fast-food place to my church, I was startled. A stranger is not really welcomed by the church's appearance. The new person would not be able to know which door worked! We certainly don't have an entrance or bathroom in the church that's accessible to those with handicaps. The bulletin wasn't even a very helpful "menu" for the service. If you didn't know how things worked, you would be lost half the time."

The insights of my students suggest some important clues for those wishing to see the body of Christ become incarnate through the ministry of local churches.

The students were very aware of the differences in motivation between the church and these businesses. We have different motives for reaching out. The fast-food stores of the world want to make money. Yet such a distinction doesn't give us much comfort. Our lofty ideals do not exempt us from failing to reach out imaginatively with the love of Christ.

Why do we make it so hard for people to come to the throne of grace? Why does the world seem to do a better job of presenting the forms of hospitality than those who have the source of genuine hospitality?

My class also read biographies of people who have built secular forms of visible communication. On each page we confronted the troubling reality that ego strength and leadership played an important role in the formation of these empires. How do these models compare to church leadership roles? We have seen so many examples of abuse by persons who seek strong leadership roles in religion, it is easy to conclude that the faith community does not need strong egos. Yet, qualities of leadership do make a difference in the way a single message becomes reality for other people.

The biblical witness reveals that God uses intentional and persistent leaders. We meet their failures as well as their successes. Yet, the elders of the tribe left a remarkable legacy of courage, risk, and conviction. They were able to draw upon both humility and confidence to fulfill their calling.

Our history as a church has been fueled by unique leaders. Yet today people in the church seem to label leaders as either ego-driven power seekers or reclusive wimps. Such extreme

judgments miss the point and are not fair to the complexity of
church leadership in our day.

My experience as a leader of more than fifteen hundred
workshops and conferences over the past twenty years has
convinced me that the local church has some of the most amazing
leaders in history, both lay and clergy. It is true that some qualify
for Reinhold Niebuhr's description of those who could model for
shirt ads. And some are simply ordinary folks who do
extraordinary acts of ministry.

Perhaps we don't need clergy in the mold of a Chuck
Yeager—independent, driven, rugged, uncompromising. Yet
the qualities of leadership should be explored by the contemporary church. What does it mean to be filled with the Spirit of God
for the ministry of the church in our day? Are our leaders running
institutions, or are they unabashedly pursuing the kingdom of
God with energy, creativity, and courage?

"Well, we have one problem." The distinguished minister got
the attention of all twenty ministers. We had been brainstorming
about how to present an engaging, lively, compelling worship
experience on television.

"We will have to rotate the preaching assignment each week.
We don't want to build a cult following around one person." I
have encountered this same conversation, with the same
statements about equality, at each of these discussions with
clergy from mainline churches. These clergy don't want another
person given the responsibility of presenting the preaching of
the church.

Yet, the secular models of communication via mass media
suggest that television demands special people who have
compelling media presence. The church needs a concept of
leadership which embraces the strength of singular gifts with the
undergirding support of the community. If our ego carries us
alone into the media maze, we will be destroyed by its energy.
No one person can handle the power generated by communicating to an audience via electronic media. The person who
conducts this energy becomes bigger than life and easily loses a
realistic sense of his or her humanity.

I believe that the faith community can "anchor" media people
in such a way that they do not forget who and whose they are. It is

the continual rehearsal of being part of the body of Christ that protects the individual from losing a sense of humility.

May God continue to lift up persons with special gifts. It is our task to affirm and extend these contributions to the work of the Kingdom. And of course, these gifts are as many in nature and as abundant among the laity as among the clergy.

The visible world offers many models and clues concerning "success." As theologians, my students have appropriately raised questions about "success" and "successful" people. These future leaders of the church have an awesome task. They must sift through the media mix for that which should be transformed by the Spirit of God and that which should be resisted. Yet, this wrestling with the invisible and visible worlds is the task that has faced the faithful of each age. Even in this electronic age when the wheat and the chaff are so confused in the culture blender, the community of faith has something special to offer.

FIVE MORE CLUES FROM THE MEDIA WORLD

1. The Receivers: Knock, Knock. Who's There?

The commercial communication system's emphasis on taking the receivers of the message very seriously is important. It is also imperative that people called to proclaim Christ understand those to whom they speak.

The communication pattern of many Christians is based either on neglecting gospel proclamation or on utilizing an aimless message without focus. Some pastors don't even know all the people in their local congregation. It is easy to assume that the people "out in the world" are the ones who face the loss of jobs, the failure of marriages, the abuse of drugs, or the problem of blending the children of two marriages. Yet, these very folks are actually sitting in front of the pastor!

We may look with justifiable criticism at the rock station that panders to the lowest common denominator of taste in its target audience. It uses consultants, contests, the phone, and interviews at concerts to explore what the listeners want. Yet, these pop communicators are strangely closer to the communication style of Jesus than are most churches. If we follow our Lord through his ministry, it is remarkable to see how many different communication modes and media he used. He preached, rebuked, told stories, used objects, debated, or simply touched others. Jesus was not cataloging communication techniques or using gimmicks. He drew upon appropriate media forms because he knew what the receivers needed in order to experience the love of God in their particular mode.

The fact that God became flesh so that we might know the saving grace of God is significant for those who focus on content but neglect the form of communication. Our media forms for the gospel should always be shaped by those who are to receive the Good News. We cannot do less than what Christ himself did for us.

This clue for ministry is probably the most revolutionary suggestion we could set before the contemporary church. It suggests that we should not prepare sermons by merely reading commentaries, finding three points, choosing stories, and wrapping it all up in a written manuscript. The pacing, immediacy, and receiver-centered communication modes of contemporary media alter our congregation. Modern media force us to realize that when we don't take our people seriously, we are actually blocking them from experiencing the power of the gospel.

"Think 27." This sign over the clock in the radio studio reminds me to picture a certain kind of person in my listening audience. We want to touch a certain share of the radio market in order to draw a definite kind of sponsor. In fact, my program director has spent a great deal of time probing the characteristics of the young adult male for whom we are programming.

The station uses an expensive consultant who provides research to support our quest to appeal to our listeners. Feedback systems and stunts are undertaken to find out more about our particular audience. The jocks are encouraged to engage the callers off the air in discussions about their hopes, dreams, and difficulties. This is done to make money and fulfill the goals of the station's owners, who are not necessarily concerned about the wellbeing of the listeners.

The church has different goals—more important ones. Yet, it does not attempt to get into the lives and minds of those to whom it directs the gospel. This needs to be changed if we are to participate in making the love of Christ visible for those who are lost in our time.

II. Risky Aggressiveness: Red Rover, Red Rover

There is also a dogged aggressiveness which marks all successful mass media efforts. "It is 90 percent hard work, 5 percent talent, and 5 percent luck." Well, the megarock star may be taking more credit than she deserves. Yet the pop media artist is just about the hardest working person in the culture. No pain, no gain.

The hard work is made up of a lot of risk. Some media artists will run in the face of corporate safety by risking it all, but too few people in the church seem to be willing to risk their security and fight to the end in their concern for bringing Christ to others.

III. Repetition: Truly, Truly

The persistence of mass media messages is also a striking clue for us. My family was approached to keep a daily log for a national television rating system. They communicated with us *seven* times, including two phone calls, and gave us a dollar (to make us feel obligated)! I have heard many church people complain because so few people came to a picnic, conference, or special service. "Why, we sent a notice to everyone in the church."

This secular message repeated seven times suggests that our single impression was not even recognized by our people. It is only after the sixth or seventh repetition that a message registers on a receiver.

This clue about persistence and redundancy gives us a major insight concerning our ability to become visible with our message of the Good News. An advertiser will buy forty television time slots on a single day when a new product is being introduced. Have you wondered why a certain television spot was played twice within five minutes? A sleepy engineer didn't make a mistake. The advertiser wanted to make an impression on the viewer.

IV. Ball of Energy and the Kitchen Sink

These attributes of mass-media communication lead us to another insight from the visible world. The successful secular communicator will try to create a ball of media energy around a message. Several different media forms may be employed to make an impact on the receiver. This will catch the attention, imagination, and response of the audience.

The economic factor which so dominates mass-media systems usually overwhelms the local Christian. What can we do without much money? It is true that some of the biggest corporations in the world control all our media systems. No rock-and-roll record can be distributed nationally without the active approval and support of the multinational companies that distribute records.

Instead of being immobilized by the power of mass media, we must take advantage of the significant points at which our common interests intersect. Where there is enormous power, there is also the possibility of drawing from it for purposes it may not originally have been designed to deliver. In other words, when the table is overflowing with abundance, it is easy to get some of it to others not at the table.

I have been amazed by the many opportunities the media power system offers people of faith. Mass-media artists love innovation and creativity and keepers of the massive media systems are not hostile to Christ and his followers. They are, however, impatient with boring programming or anything that will lose the audience.

If the gospel is presented in a boring manner not in keeping with its natural vitality and power, it doesn't deserve to be communicated. It is an insult to Christ to use old wineskins for the new wine. The high standards of creativity and interest demanded by the secular media systems are proper. They are calling us to be faithful to the content of our message.

V. Pervasiveness: Here, There, and Everywhere

A fifth clue from the visible media systems in the media world is its pervasiveness. The messages, desirable or not, creep into every part of our lives. If others can get to people with their messages, can we not use the same methods to bring Christ to them?

As you have gathered, I am twisting the message of despair, which fills so many media books, into moments of hope and promise. I am optimistic because of my twenty-year personal experience as a servant of Christ in the media mix. I promise that there never have been as many opportunities for presenting Christ through media forms as there are today. The road to such faithfulness is paved with difficulties, risks, failures—and endless joy.

I hope this book is in the hands of someone who never has undertaken the kinds of challenges offered here. If you are inexperienced, great! You will not be tainted by the stories of hopelessness that the prophets of doom have proclaimed to those doing media.

The plans, dreams, and ideas on these pages are possible sources of hope and practical results for you and your people. The probes have emerged from many different people who so love God and their people that they will do anything to bring the two together.

I invite you to face the visible world, with its awesome media systems, as you serve the community of faith.

AND SO . . .

We are swimming in a media environment. The modern media forms seep into our being. There is no escape from their influences and abuses. Yet God sets us free to transform the corrupt messages into moments of grace and love.

We are called to learn from the moment we are placed for ministry. Our critical sense of false messages does not need to blind us from the possibility of using the same electronic doorways to proclaim Christ. The visible church and the visible world are inseparably bound in texture, if not in substance. Our wondrous task is to transform the communication moments and modes into occasions for the proclamation of the gospel.

Chapter 4

THE PARTY:
A MODEL FOR
EVANGELISM OUTREACH

THE KIT AND KABOODLE

"I wish someone would put together something to help the local church get as many people at worship on Pentecost Sunday as on Easter Sunday." There was a brief silence. Then the room exploded with excitement. Everyone was talking at once. The immediate response to John's suggestion made the roomful of religious communication leaders sound like characters from an Andy Hardy movie. Remember? Mickey Rooney would come up with an idea for the kids to put on a show in the barn, and Judy Garland was ready to sing and dance. This kind of let's-do-it spirit is infrequent in most church committee meetings. Yet something special was about to take place for that church.

This spark burst into flame a few weeks later as a group of local church representatives from around the country met to dream and plan. The Party was the result of that quest for a holistic outreach to celebrate the birthday of the church. This dream would become a great blessing to the fourteen hundred churches that used the plan.

GOALS

The plan developed in a Florida motel room had three goals:

1. To focus the spiritual energy of the local congregations.
2. To raise the awareness in the local communities of the faithfulness of the Presbyterian Church to the gospel.
3. To bring as many people to worship on Pentecost Sunday as on Easter Sunday.

The committee (Betty Redman, David Cassie, James Boos, and Bill Guilford) decided to develop a kit that would provide resources for a congregation of one hundred or more. The kit would be built on insights from the world of secular media and the best of historical theology.

The general concern of the committee was evangelism. This is a vast area of ministry. We knew we could not create a whole plan which provided training and follow-up. It was also assumed that our churches generally had little recent experience in aggressive evangelism. In fact, many people in the denomination misunderstood the theology of evangelism and actually opposed it!

It was our contention that a successful single event would nudge most churches into a more sympathetic view of evangelism. How could each person feel affirmation through the ministry of outreach? How could we combine the biblical promise with the perceived needs of those outside the faith community?

Our understanding of the biblical injunction to be angels or messengers of the Good News embraced both spiritual and incarnational Good News. In other words, we are called to provide both the message and the experience of Jesus Christ with others. For us there is no separation between feeding the physical and feeding the spiritual hungers of those who need Christ. It was this incarnational conviction that drove us into the evangelism plan.

THE PLAN

The second chapter of Acts provided the blueprint for this program. We quickly realized that there was nothing we could develop for the celebration of Pentecost that would be more extreme than the historical event itself! God utilized the rushing wind, flames of fire, and a message that all could understand.

We could emphasize only limited aspects of the gospel in this single program of outreach, so we decided that in this initial act of evangelism, we wanted to help the stranger experience the hospitality of Christ. This theological gift is more than friendliness. It is built on the biblical theme of *nephesh*, or community spirit, which existed in Old Testament times. Abraham and Sarah took in strangers who appeared at their door.

They offered the safety and hospitality of their tent, and in response to this act, the angels revealed their message about the aged couple's impending parenthood.

This same spirit of hospitality can be found in the New Testament. When the disciples invited a stranger to join them at table on the road to Emmaus, the resurrected Christ was revealed to them.

When we embrace the stranger with love and acceptance, we invite the presence of the Spirit. The disciples were together in a room when the Spirit gave birth to the church. The Greek text is laden with words which indicate that they were "together." It is this state of hospitality that is central to the proclamation of the gospel.

ORGANIZATION

How could we help the local congregations prepare to embrace the stranger? Many church communities are not really disposed to incorporate the stranger into their midst. The newcomer, or babe in Christ, always changes the nature of the existing community. It is the babe in the faith who raises the simplest questions. Of course those basic inquiries can be triggers that release the Good News, invitations to recite our history of salvation. In fact, it is always the host and hostess who are blessed by the stranger at the table.

It seemed that prayer, Bible study, and witnessing were key preparations for hosting the birthday party for the church. The journey from Easter Sunday to Pentecost Sunday would be a time of spiritual readiness. An experiential daily devotional series was developed for The Party and placed in each kit. Here are sample entries from four days:

DAY 1.
Read James 1:9-11. Find a blade of grass or leaf from a plant or tree.

REFLECTION EXERCISE. Write about the blessings of a time when you were poor, and the curses when you were richer.

_____

_____

_____

BECOMING THE WORD. Affix the leaf to your lapel or blouse. Wear it out in public today. Write about the discussions you had today with people about the curse of depending on materialism when they ask about the leaf.

_____

_____

_____

_____

_____

DAY 2.

Read James 1:12. You need a pencil and paper. Also buy a sheet of the stars used to reward students. They can be found in school-supply sections.

REFLECTION EXERCISE. Draw a crown with six points. Label each "star" or point with an example of a personal trial. Write about how God has blessed you through them.

_____

_____

_____

_____

_____

BECOMING THE WORD. Put a star on the back of the hand or on the watch of each person you meet today. Tell them that is to remind them that God is blessing them—even during hard times. Write about your experiences with this ministry of blessing.

_____

_____

_____

_____

_____

DAY 3.

Read James 3:1-5. Bring a wooden lead pencil to your devotion time.

REFLECTION EXERCISE. Put the "bit" (pencil) between your teeth. Think about the worst thing you ever said to someone. What happened as the result of an unbridled tongue? Write about this story from your life.

_____

_____

_____

_____

_____

BECOMING THE WORD. Today carry the pencil with you. When you talk with others, hold it in your hand. When you feel tempted to respond impulsively, put the eraser to your lips first as a reminder to listen with love. What changed when you controlled your tongue with others?

_____

_____

_____

_____

_____

DAY 4.

Read James 4:8-9. You will need a bar of soap.

REFLECTION EXERCISE. Rub your hands with the soap. Smell the bar. Write about the dirty parts of your life that need to be washed away.

_____

_____

_____

_____

_____

BECOMING THE WORD. Choose one of the sins discussed above. Live today in the reality that God has washed away your sin through Jesus Christ. What will you do differently today? How is your life changed by this fact? Write about this experience.

_____

_____

_____

_____

_____

We urged the members of the leadership teams to accept this discipline as a way to prepare themselves for the special day. Many churches encouraged as many of their members as possible to undertake this daily study and activity. One church had three hundred people involved. Each Sunday the people who were doing the study gathered, and during the worship service they shared what had happened to them as a result of prayer, Bible study, and living the passage with other people each day.

The kit also contained a general guide for planning The Party. We were careful to suggest the general structure without filling in too many details. The Party could be successful only if it became the genuine outreach of the congregation.

Some congregations took a year to plan the celebration, while others did it in three weeks! The key to The Party's success was the involvement of 30 to 40 percent of their members in the planning. It was amazing how easy it was to get people to work on a specific project. It is when we ask people to serve on a committee forever that they balk.

Participation also breeds excitement. People began to be proud of what they were designing, and this nudged them to invite others to the service. Evangelism succeeds when people are proud of their church and its program.

MEDIA

In addition to a general plan, The KIT eventually contained a resource book with more than eighty ideas developed by the local churches themselves. Here are some of the wonderful things created by congregations all over the country as they sought to make the love of Christ visible to others.

1. Twelve-foot banners were stretched across the highway in front of one church. The banners featured the same art that appeared on bumper stickers made for the occasion ("Come to The Party").

2. Another church printed three-foot copies of the red flame and stapled them to stakes. These were given to members of the congregation, who placed them in their front yards. On

Pentecost Sunday they were brought and placed in front of the church.

3. The shut-ins of a congregation were given the names of people who had been married, baptized, or had a family member die during the past twenty years. They called the people on the list and invited them to church on Pentecost Sunday for the service and a church dinner. Long-absent folks were delighted with this personal invitation.

4. A cluster of churches in a Presbytery purchased space (very reasonably) for a series of newspaper advertisements. They created a "teaser" campaign which evoked the curiosity of the reader. The small ads were scattered throughout the paper, with questions such as "Are you lonely?" "Looking for friends?" The final ad invited them to The Party at the participating churches.

5. Lapel buttons bearing the logo of the denomination were given out on Easter Sunday. Members and visitors were told that the tomb was empty and Christ had risen. However, God was going to do still more when he gave birth to the church! Everyone was told to join in witnessing for Christ during the following six weeks by wearing the buttons. Each Sunday, at a given point in the service, they would be asked to share what had happened to them as they wore the button during the previous week.

One elder wasn't quite sure how he felt about wearing a lapel button. He tried it out by wearing it to the bank where he worked. He called to say that within the first hour two people asked him about the button. "You know what happened when I told them that I was an elder in a Presbyterian church? They told me their problems and I was able to minister to them!" This man became a key supporter of The Party in that church.

Many people have found the lapel buttons a real blessing as others asked about the flame. However, one woman reported that she was blessed by wearing it. Her daughter was ill in the hospital. On her way to visit the young girl a doctor spoke to her in the elevator. "I see your button. You are a Presbyterian. So am I." The doctor asked why she was there, and after hearing about her daughter, he got off the elevator with her, visited the child, and they prayed together. He said he would drop in on the girl from time to time. "It was so good to know that another Presbyterian was there."

At one church, the members refused to let bumper stickers be placed on their cars. The minister explained to the congregation the important role the bumper stickers played in raising the awareness of the community to their church. He promised that the following Saturday, he would wash all the cars that bore bumper stickers!

6. Presbyterian and Methodist churches sit side by side in one Pennsylvania town. They decided to celebrate Pentecost together as a united witness in the community, so they combined their slogans: "Come to The Party and Catch the Spirit."

7. A small-town church prepared for The Party by organizing a clown ministry troupe, basing their performance on the liturgy for Pentecost Sunday. With a huge banner and a truck decorated with announcements about The Party celebration at the church, the troupe went through their town on a mission of ministry. They stopped at various points and provided moments of clowning for groups of people along the street.

8. Invitations were printed and sent through the inexpensive postage option which delivers mailings to each household. This was used as part of the total community program.

9. Another church organized five separate task groups to prepare for The Party: devotional, publicity, dinner planning, worship, and hospitality. They found that people would accept responsibility to serve for a specific period of time at a particular task. "Can you bake a birthday cake for The Party?"

10. A new church development noted that the people in their community enjoyed the cooking of a noted chef in their town. He was invited to prepare an incomparable barbecue, and the whole community was invited to The Party. The attendance on Pentecost Sunday set a record—three times the number of people worshiped on that day than on any previous Sunday!

11. Another small-town church placed banners over the highway which runs past their church. When they decided to roast a pig for The Party dinner, it was learned that they would need to start the cooking process the night before Pentecost

Sunday. A huge fire was lighted on the front yard of the church, and they were amazed when strangers stopped all through the night. It was a great time for personal evangelism and ministry.

12. During the Pentecost Worship, everyone was asked to take out the pew Bible and open to any passage. When the congregation was asked to read the passages aloud at the same time, they experienced the confusion of tongues.

13. Another church asked eights folks from different countries to read the Scripture, each in a different language. The pastor then read the second chapter of Acts in English.

14. Red geraniums decorated every space in the sanctuary of many churches. The blazing color added greatly to the flame image of the Scripture passage.

15. Small whistles which made a whirling sound were used by many congregations, especially in connection with the reading from Acts about the great wind at the birth moment of the church.

16. Everybody seemed to use balloons for the celebration of this special day. One church had hundreds of balloons with long red ribbons, hanging from the ceiling. The streams represented the flames of fire. After the service, the balloons were released in the parking lot.

17. One Sunday school class made small flames with construction paper and mounted them on paper straws. During the reading of the passages in Acts they waved them over their heads like flags.

18. Signing for the deaf was used in several churches for the reading of the passage. This is a very meaningful and moving means of communication.

19. At one church the people in charge of The Party solved the problem of getting people to stay for the meal following worship by having the whole congregation process out of the sanctuary and into the fellowship hall for the benediction. They all stayed!

20. Many churches had reunions on Pentecost Sunday. One asked everyone to wear the same style of clothing worn the last time they went to Sunday school. Former members were invited

from many different states. There was standing room only that
day at worship!

21. A West Coast pastor borrowed makeup and costume from
friends in the local community drama group, dressed as Peter,
and gave a first-person sermon.

22. One couple began their special personal evangelism on
Pentecost Sunday. They began to invite visitors at church home
for dinner each week! They were surprised that most people
accepted, and many stayed on to become members.

23. One church gave each person present a silver dollar, to be
used to take someone out for coffee or food in order to witness to
Jesus Christ. The stories of their outreach in this manner were
shared at the next worship service. Many touching stories were
told the following week.

The one hundred lapel buttons included in the kit contained a
white flame, taken from the logo of the denomination. We knew
that many folks did not have the recent experience of witnessing
to others. They wouldn't wear something that stated an overt
religious message. This "teaser" approach meant that others
might ask the wearer about the button and give our people a
chance to witness.

Only fifteen bumper stickers were included, since we knew
that many folks do not want such stickers on their cars. Yet, even
fifteen stickers could make an amazing impact on a single town.
We chose removable ones, and many churches had the young
people put them on cars (with the owners' permission) after
Sunday morning worship.

A packet of eight newspaper advertisements was included in the
kits. This was the most frequently utilized mass medium.
Churches found many creative ways to use the local papers. Many
newspapers would almost trade paid ads for editorial articles.

An intellectual course on evangelism was also included in the
kit. Many churches used this study to guide them through the
Bible in the quest to understand evangelism. The content of the
gospel as outreach is vital to this model. We must know whose we
are, if we want to share the fruits of the faith with others.

Many pastors used their computers to keep in touch with the

preparation for The Party in other parts of the country. Computers were used in a couple areas as a means of contacting people who had fallen away from the church in the past few years. The names were listed, and they were sent special invitations to the celebration.

AFTERWARD

The evaluation sheets from the churches that participated in The Party indicated that each had more people at worship than on the previous Pentecost Sunday. Many had more than had attended the Easter service, and some had more than at any time in the history of their church! One region of seventy-five participating churches was polled concerning the presence of visitors for The Party. They found that more than 600 new people were present on Pentecost Sunday! One church had 175 people on Easter Sunday, but more than 370 on Pentecost.

However, it was the report of the spiritual blessings received by both members and strangers, which touched us most deeply. Lives were changed during the development of the event and by the Spirit of God experienced on Pentecost. Many people talked about the crowded building, the power of the hymns, the inspired preaching, and the deep sense of God's presence in the hospitality that flowed among strangers and members.

"Our preacher got caught up in the Spirit, deserted his manuscript, and preached the gospel to us!"

"I hugged people I had not seen in years!"

"Tears streamed down my face as I felt the Spirit of God descending upon our church."

"A new young family approached me after the service. The father said 'How am I going to explain to my children that every Sunday won't be as exciting as today?' "

Most of the evaluations were done by lay people. It was very moving to hear about their blessings experienced at The Party. Many thanked us for helping them discover Pentecost Sunday as a gift from God.

You don't need any information except that included in this chapter to celebrate Pentecost in a visible way. Just make the second chapter of Acts visible in your congregation and encourage others to share it. Through it, you will not only enliven your congregation, you will also be using these concepts from the mass media world.

1. The Party was *holistic*. Both group media (the way folks communicate among themselves) and mass-media forms were used to create its energy. All the approaches kept coming back to the purpose of the event. No one media form carried the whole event.

"I am sorry to write that The Party did not work for us. I sat and waited for the television spots to bring people in." This confession indicates that this pastor had not understood the inclusive nature of this manifestation of the visible church as outreach. Television, radio, and newspapers alone do not bring people to the community of faith. Advertising can only tease, beckon, or give a taste of what needs to be fully experienced within the body of Christ. It was the singular work of those who hosted The Party in response to Christ that made it work.

2. The Party was *redundant in its outreach*. Those who received the most out of this model were those who went out again and again to the community to make multiple impressions about the event. These local evangelists didn't write just one letter or make one announcement. They persistently battered the community from many different directions, until a critical mass of input broke through into the consciousness of the receivers of the message.

3. The Party was *a bonding of form and content*. The people who made this program such a smashing success continually drew upon the message of the gospel in Acts 2 as the source of their model for the visible church. It is this link which kept The Party from being a series of gimmicks. These folks prayed, studied the Bible, witnessed, and risked, in order that others might know the healing and saving grace of God.

4. The Party was *a program* triggered by enabling *clergy leadership*. Pastors functioned almost like mass-media producers, the persons who combine all the pieces of talent and resources. He or she utilizes the great talents of others.

5· The Party *recycled existing resources* into a new meaningful totality. It found a point of mutual need in the mass-media community and used this symbiotic relationship to create powerful alliances between church and media.

6. The Party proved that the church can provide the resources it needs for something it values.

AND SO . . .

This model can be used by your congregation. The birthday of the church is a special gift from God, a special time when God calls together strangers and others to praise the wondrous works of our Creator. For congregations that have not previously made the faith visible to others in intentional ways, this is an excellent first step toward the incarnational act.

Of course, by itself, this is not a holistic evangelism program. It lacks serious and ongoing study. There is no suggested follow-up program with the visitors. However, The Party is a special opportunity for the visible church. Once the people of God experience the success and blessings of their outreach in the name of Christ, they will never again be the same.

Chapter 5

THE 200 CLUB:
A MODEL FOR
FIGHTING DRUG ABUSE

"We were worried. There was so much talk in the papers about young people using drugs in our community." This Christian woman's concern represents more than just another private murmuring about sin. She and her friends placed their fear before Christ. The answer they received was built on their confidence in young people. They chose not to warn the youths about drugs or threaten them with the dangers.

"We knew we must stand with them as they make their own decisions." From this important foundation, these folks designed the 200 Club.

They invited each of the six-graders in their church for a personal interview with a committee of adults. The young people were invited to join the 200 Club. Each year they would be asked to make a covenant with God in the presence of the people of God. They would promise that they would not use drugs or alcohol during the next year.

If they lived by this commitment, they would be enrolled in a program that would earn each one a $200 savings bond upon graduation from high school. The adults raised the money for the bonds by selling baked goods and by other fund-raising events. In the several years since the program, all the committed students have kept their vows.

This is a very significant model for the visible church. These folks are standing with young people as they make the choice to walk with Jesus. Joe Paterno, Penn. State football coach, reports that he uses drug testing with athletes because the students need the support of the coach's firmness. When someone at a party offers one of their team members a drug, the athlete can use the coach's position to back him up: "Coach will test me." There are times when young people need this kind of support from significant adults. Let's take this fine program and add the perspective of the visible church.

GOALS

1. To support youth in their Christian decision concerning drugs and alcohol.
2. To focus the supportive energy of the community on this important problem.
3. To raise the awareness in the community of your church's faith as it touches the whole person.

Then let's expand this excellent concept. Peer ministry training focuses on equipping young people to care for those around them. They listen to and care for friends who are having difficulty. Of course, this ministry of youth to youth extends care in a way that adults simply can't hope to accomplish. Most young people turn to other young people for advice and help in their problems. Peer ministry provides young people with training and support to meet others in their problems and difficulties. It enables them to bring those with serious needs to adults who can give professional help.

The concept of enabling youth to minister is at the very heart of the gospel, which calls believers, young and old, to be servants of Jesus Christ. Such a program requires that a select group of people covenant to meet regularly. These meetings focus on prayer, reports of encounters with people since the last meeting, and reflection with a significant adult. Some groups even keep journals or share written accounts of actual encounters with particular persons. This case-study approach adds a great deal.

Practicing the faith in life situations with the support of the church enables Christians to grow as spiritual persons. In other words, there is nothing more helpful in strengthening a young Christian's decision about drug abuse than working with others who may be tempted. This approach works with the help of a trained adult who can encourage the youths in those demanding moments of ministry.

Another way to build a program that gives young Christians maximum support as they live their vows concerning drugs is the use of a personal support person. Many alcohol rehabilitation programs utilize this technique. A recovering alcoholic is provided with a person who can be called day or night for help in moments of temptation. The recovering person must carry change for a phone call at all times.

THE PLAN

What if this concept were incorporated in the 200 Club program? The bonding between a youth and an adult can be a very significant relationship of mutual ministry.

Years ago I was a Good Humor salesman. I drove a big white truck and dispensed frozen goodies to children in the streets of Detroit. It was the only summer job I could get, and I needed every cent for my impending marriage in the fall.

Being the newest kid with the company, I filled in for the other guys when they took a day off. I was forced to take the worst trucks, and they always seemed to stall. The refrigerated unit was loaded with a chemical substance that would lose its cool after a long day. This could mean that the ice cream would get soft by the end of a twelve-hour day.

Selling ice cream is a strange experience. One dispenses the highest sensual delight for young children, so they tend to idolize the driver as the giver of great joy. I remember one hot afternoon on a suburban street. A huge gang of neighborhood children had gathered around the truck, and I had passed out the iced goodies to everyone. Then I waved good-bye and jumped into the open cab.

I tried again and again, but the truck would not even turn over! I knew the repair truck would take hours to get there. I stood up and shrugged my shoulders.

The children came streaming around the cab. They were cheering, "The Good Humor man is going to stay on our street." "We can have ice cream all day!"

I told them I would love to stay in their neighborhood, but I was going to be married in a couple of weeks, and I needed to sell my ice cream along the whole route in order to get the money I needed. There was a strange silence.

I was feeling sorry for myself and trying to figure out what to do when I noticed something funny was happening. My truck was rocking!

I jumped out and went to the back of the vehicle. Fifteen children were trying to push my truck, their faces in deep concentration!

I was deeply moved by their care. I explained that they were not strong enough to move the heavy truck fast enough to get it started.

A few minutes later, one child brought a teenage brother, who jumped the battery and got me on my way. I drove down the street with the cheers of those special young people ringing in my ears.

That kind of mutual care could be reflected in the 200 Club. Each young person could receive a support person who would walk with him or her during the next year of the covenant. They would contact each other every week, or more frequently if necessary. This bonding between youth and adult would provide the kind of Christian community that would make the journey of responsible decision making significant for both.

Much has been said about the damaging influence of some peers on young people (and on adults). Some people are influenced negatively because the faith community has failed to be a place where peers can form significant relationships. A vital youth group can have the same kind of peer bonding as a group of friends from non-Christian settings. The need to have significant others is basic and important. The 200 Club provides an amazing focus for the community of faith to be a communion of faith.

The visible church seeks to make the faith incarnate as it takes expression in life. Its quest is to touch both the internal community and the external world. This is not "public relations." That concept has most often been utilized for hype or false building up of the attributes of an institution or a person. There is a boasting gait to such public posture. While we have no choice but to make visible the love of Christ to others, and any means should be considered in our outreach, all those means or media should lift up only authentic moments of the Christian life.

The 200 Club is one of those extremely important moments in which vital attributes of living in Christ are being manifested. It is a perfect program for making the ministry of Christ visible to the secular community.

Parents and significant adults are extremely important in youth programming. Be sure to work them into your version of this program and also into the covenant worship service for those taking the drug-free vow.

THE WORSHIP SERVICE

Contact the resources in your community that are also interested in a preventive approach to chemical abuse. Most of the money and time in this field is spent on treatment or enforcement of laws. These aspects are very important, but the faith community's greatest message is the power of the gospel to strengthen a person facing temptation. This preventive power is very special and differs from many secular approaches.

The local, state, and national law enforcement agencies will be cooperative. It will be easy to invite officials from each of the agencies to the covenant worship service. Design the service in such a way that one or more of those officials can share their support for the program publicly.

You will also find that the institutions hardest hit by drug abuse will be very cooperative. For instance, the professional sports world is very responsive to preventive drug programs. Coaches and players have very willingly made themselves available for our syndicated weekly radio program, "Winners."

"Len Bias was my hero. He gave me hope that I might also excel in sports. I just hoped that my work at sports would help me to meet him someday. I was destroyed by his death. I want to think that he only tried drugs once."

The disillusionment and confusion of this teenage female track star is the kind of impact most professional athletes want to change. What if you invited local sports figures to join in making the same vows as the young people! They could become partners for the year in supporting each other. The public statement of this process would make a huge impact on the community.

The mass media will love this program. Involve them early. They will have news makers (officials and sports people) offering something special. With each report, you offer a visible sign that the church of Jesus Christ is faithful to its call.

People will begin to associate your church with an important public service. It will not seem self-serving, which often emerges in the advertising of church services on the religion page. Mass media publicity notices about our congregational events often have an insular feeling which suggests that we are talking only to our own. Or we seem to say, with our pancake supper announcement, "Let's have this community pay for our programming."

The covenant worship service can be special. There is always time during the worship of God to deal seriously with faith journeys. I am always saddened when congregations will baptize or christen as many children and families as possible on a given Sunday. Such a practice seems to suggest that we want to hose them down and get them out of the way as quickly as possible.

Every worship experience should be special. Each time the people of faith praise God, it is personal and important. The sense of specialness also reminds the weekly worshipers that their gospel is worthy and that they can invite strangers with a sense of pride and expectation.

When we study the covenant ceremonies of the Bible, a helpful pattern emerges. For instance, in Joshua 24 we meet the tribes of ancient Israel as they are confronted with a decision. Joshua challenges them to follow Yahweh. "As for me and my family, we choose the Lord." The tribes responded that they chose Yahweh.

There are implications in such a decision. People are expected to keep the way of the Lord. The Lord is part of the covenant, and God will be faithful. There are also implications if the covenant is broken.

Joshua knew that humans are prone to forget their commitments. If we can't see or touch a reality, how will it remain present? How do we make visible what we have experienced in an invisible manner?

Joshua asked the people to focus on a rock. "May this stone remind you of what you promised here!" Wherever there is a covenant ceremony in the Bible, we usually find there is a tangible or visible way by which it can be remembered. ("As often as you eat and drink, do this in remembrance of me").

Perhaps you could draw upon this passage for your 200 Club worship service. Each person taking the vows would be given a symbol to help him or her remember what had been promised. The stone of Joshua could be the perfect object. Perhaps a lapidary, a person who polishes stones, could help by transforming some pebbles into shiny stones. The youths would carry these each day as personal choices are made and the ministry of caring for peers is undertaken.

These shiny covenant stones could also be used as the focus of reflection in the group meetings. Each week another Scripture passage which refers to stones could be the center of the Bible study! Each person's stone would take on additional meaning. Sometimes the stones could be exchanged, with the instruction that every day at lunch, each youth would pray for the person whose stone he or she carried. At the next meeting, they could share what it is like to know that someone is intentionally praying for you.

Special music, special guests (relatives of the people taking vows), special prayers, and guest speakers can make this a memorable service for the Christians making this decision. The church stands with its younger members as they decide to be servants of Jesus Christ in a specific aspect of their lives.

It is important to provide an intentional climate of hospitality so that all who are present experience the visible church. You may serve a dinner after the service to which everyone present is invited. Simplicity, warmth, and excellent food can make this a special time for being the church. The guests will add a great deal, and members will have the opportunity to congratulate those taking the vows.

It is also important for those who have taken the vows to be able to share their experiences occasionally with the whole church. They can testify to what is happening in their lives and in the lives of others. This will bless the congregation and be helpful to the participants in the 200 Club.

MEDIA

It will also be vital that you or the committee that supports the 200 Club keep thinking about the visible church. There should be calls to the local press and electronic media every few weeks, with information about the program and the participants. You will quickly develop a warm relationship with contact people. They will grow to trust you and accept your judgment about whether something is newsworthy. You will need to earn this trust, but it will be a relationship that will be a blessing both to your church and to the media people. There is an opportunity for a chaplaincy to the media in this process. Don't underrate a trusting relationship with those folks, who are under enormous pressure.

You may want to launch your 200 Club publicly by calling a press conference a few days before the covenant Sunday. This can be done by contacting local media with a printed press release; call them with a reminder. Feature one of the celebrities or young people at the conference. Check the appendix section for details on how to organize a press conference.

The creators of media love human-interest stories, and the church is the community of stories. We are Christians only because our forbears told how God worked in their lives and the lives of those who went before them. The biggest problem facing mass media is that they have run out of stories. There is no content for their communication forms. Reporters, producers, and talk-show hosts have no problem talking about the religious foundation of the 200 Club. They usually are looking for any item genuinely newsworthy—that is—interesting to the viewer.

There is another challenging dimension to this program, which would require special interest and commitment. Your church could host a weekly radio talk show on chemical abuse. I have conducted such a program for almost twenty years—the station even paid me to host it. It won national awards, had a huge audience, and drew over six thousand letters. One cannot counsel, heal, or convert over the radio. However, that show modeled a preevangelism experience which led many to seek counseling help.

Your young people might be willing to be guests on various talk shows every few months. That would keep the program before the public and help your 200 Club participants remain strong through the recital of their vows. Radio stations will be very helpful.

The computer also could play an important role in your program. For instance, lists of resources could be gathered from billboards and other sources that deal with chemical abuse. There probably are members of your congregation who can help you develop a list of supporters for your drug program.

If you start a newsletter, you can weave participants and supporters together. The computer can be a great help with desk-top publishing, address labels, and subscribers. The material gathered from the journals of participants can be shared through this print piece.

And So . . .

This holistic program of ministry is extremely challenging and inviting for the local church. I assure you that it can be a blessing to all involved. Several important strengths for the visible church are contained in this model:

1. It will enable your people to present a visible witness, which teaches a great deal about the redeeming and guiding power of Jesus Christ in people's lives.

2. The plan demonstrates that our visible witness in the world must be based on some authentic form of ministry which teaches by its very nature and that it is being shared as a sign to the world.

3. The 200 Club also shows that the immediate problems which confront every community are really opportunities to do what the church has always been called upon to do. There is no problem or difficulty in our culture that is not an opportunity for witness and ministry. The visible church's incarnational view of the gospel acknowledges no separation between the spiritual realm and the behavioral realm.

4. This model also offers an image of young people as faithful witnesses. The ministry of youth is one of the neglected aspects of local church ministry. The struggles of teens are often seen as something they will simply pass through until they reach the only important stage of the Christian life—adulthood.

5. The plan also demonstrates how mass media forms can be marshaled to help the ministry of the local church.

6. Last, the 200 Club offers a model for the way a holistic approach can create a critical impact upon the local church and the community it serves.

Chapter 6

THE PEACE PUZZLE: A MODEL FOR THE VISIBLE CHURCH

"Zap!" The futuristic sound came from the strange looking laser gun held by the young child. The expression on his face was frozen in intense agony. He had become one of the avenging superheroes of television. Eddie had me in his sights as he vaporized me.

There is much talk among Christians about the need for peace. Many in the faith community have drawn upon the rich legacy of peacemaking that is an inseparable part of the gospel. Most people who follow the Prince of Peace acknowledge that justice and peace as reconciliation are known most fully in the life, death, and resurrection of Jesus Christ. The cross stands as an enduring sign of our responsibility.

Yet much of our lives is spent facing signs of death, alienation, and destruction. A child wielding an imagined instrument of death is merely a sign of the times. Television offers daily glimpses of battleships, rumbling tanks, weary soldiers, and angry terrorists.

Across our living rooms and into our brains creep unforgettable images. Weeping parents hold the body of a baby killed by a bomb. Brave mothers from Central America dance with pictures of missing husbands and sons pinned to their dresses. The names of the nations and people change with each report, but the lack of peace is ever present.

It has been hard for the people of God to focus on the divine imperative to be peacemakers. Thee has been a tendency to become internally distracted about the means of bringing peace. Christians are hard on one another as they debate. Even active peacemakers are critical about the way others are seeking peace in the community. It is the *how* of peacemaking that gives the faith community such unrest. How do we live the peace of God in our complex times?

THE PLAN

The Peace Puzzle is a plan that arose in the Pittsburgh area through the interest of Presbyterians and Catholics. How could they provide a devotional experience on a foundation that would include all ages and prepare a way to witness for peace in the larger community?

Ruth Rylander is an active peacemaker who contributed a great deal to this model. She has shared her life and calling with people across the country. "My daughter was in high school when she contracted a virulent type of leukemia. When I visited her in the hospital before her death, I was confronted by a ward of young people who had lost their hair, had their bodies covered with bruises, and were facing death. I was suddenly reminded of the death camps of World War II. It seemed they were saying to me that the whole world was dying. I felt that God was calling me to dedicate my life to peacemaking."

How could we be inclusive in our presentation of peacemaking? We knew that Christ gave us no option about this aspect of discipleship. He calls us to be ambassadors of reconciliation.

We looked first at the receivers of this ministry opportunity. Our analysis quickly revealed that local church members were the obvious focus of our message. Why should they want to undertake a peace study? What were their perceived needs? When does the local congregation seem most open to focus on special concerns? Christmas came to our attention immediately! The Christmas season raised the concern for peace in a natural way.

The church always needs programming for this time of year, and the coming of the Christ Child creates the perfect atmosphere for the consideration of peace. It is also an important time for Christian families.

However, we realized that families within the church often had a problem with the Christmas season. Many parents disliked the commercial frenzy stimulated by toy stores and television advertising. Greed and visions of toys and other gifts threatened to dominate many families. Further examination revealed that many families had never developed a meaningful devotional pattern. Parents somehow had failed to establish a Bible study and sharing format which would have made the gospel a central part of the family. How could we meet this important need with our message of peacemaking?

It was decided that we would focus on the family table as the setting for family devotions around the theme of peacemaking. We hoped most families had at least one meal together each day. This would provide a special opportunity.

Old and New Testament texts which dealt with different aspects of peace were chosen, and twenty-five exercises based on these texts were written. These devotional activities were holistic opportunities in which all ages could participate equally, and we urged families to invite single friends to their table during this season. An artist designed a three-dimensional dove of heavy cardboard which could be cut out and stapled together. The devotional exercises were printed on "feathers" which could be stored along the wing of the dove.

The dove, with its "feathers," was then placed on the table as a centerpiece. Each night during Advent, the four weeks before Christmas, a member of the table group would take a feather from the dove and lead the rest through an exercise. Here are some of the exercises:

1. Read James 3:17-18 aloud. Pass a saltshaker around the table. Shake a few grains into each person's hand. Ask diners to tell how this ancient substance symbolizes wisdom and righteousness. Close with circle prayer, asking each person to include the word *wisdom*.

2. Read John 14:27 aloud. Invite each person to pick up a spoon and look into its shiny surface. Ask each diner to share the way its dull reflection symbolizes something troubling about his or her life. Close with a prayer circle focusing on praise for the peace and comfort promised by Christ. (Invite someone to the next night's dinner, and decorate the table to welcome the guest.)

3. *Read Romans 15:7-13 aloud.* Give each person a toothpick (or pass around a small stick). Let each person share how the wood (the root of Jesse) relates to Christ and his gifts. Close with a joyous prayer circle for the guest.

4. *Read Isaiah 14:5-7 aloud.* Tear a page from a newspaper or magazine for each person. Let each person at the table share a story or picture from the paper which expresses the promise of God's justice against pride and arrogance. Close with a prayer circle, focusing on God's power over oppression.

5. *Read Psalm 33:16-36 aloud.* Pass a small mirror around the table. Ask each person to share thoughts about whether that reflection was the person's true reflection in God's sight. What shield does God provide? Conclude with a prayer circle focusing on the protection of faith for each person.

6. *Read Romans 5:1-11 aloud.* Have each person stand and touch the next person's shoulder. Encourage each one to say a blessing for the person touched that emerges from the Romans passage. Close with a prayer circle of thanksgiving for the gift of the Christ child.

7. *Read Luke 2:1-20 aloud.* Pass around a baby blanket. Ask each person to share the thoughts Mary and Joseph must have felt as they held their child. What thoughts come to mind? Does the lack of peace around us take away from this Advent moment? Close with a prayer circle for all those outside this circle of grace.

The dove and Bible exercises were placed in an attractive envelope, along with a list of special Christmas services. These Peace Puzzle packets were distributed to the Presbyterian and Catholic churches of the area. In some churches the worshipers received three or four packets and were urged to take them to their neighbors as gifts and invite them to the church for the Christmas season. People seemed to be quite comfortable in offering this devotional material to friends and to strangers. For many of our people this was the first step to door visitation on behalf of the gospel. The kits were received with enthusiasm.

We struggled with the inclusive dimension to biblical peacemaking. Churches have reported that peacemaking materials from the national denominations often caused problems when used in local settings. So much of the material focused on the number of weapons, the dangers of nuclear stockpiles, and the like. Of course, these are all part of the war problem. Yet Jesus is demanding an even more radical obedience in our ministry of reconciliation. Such an understanding of peace touches every part of life. Couldn't every single person be reached as a follower of the Prince of Peace, if the quest for peace were placed in an inclusive perspective?

We finally developed a study process which reflected our view. A large felt dove was created which could be taken apart like a puzzle. We developed several ways this resource could be used.

One of our favorite ways to use this Peace Puzzle dove was to explain to a group that each piece represented one of these kinds of peace: domestic-family, economic, justice, racial, international, political, personal, military. Each of the eight pieces was placed on a different table, and the people were asked to choose the piece they could most comfortably affirm.

This inclusive process pulls together just about every group of people. Every person could accept a part of peace as his or her responsibility. Our role as peacemakers of Jesus Christ is to include as many brothers and sisters as possible. We are not called to seek correct theology and political philosophy, but to be spiritually faithful to our Lord.

We also produced several tapes of Ruth Rylander's journey to peacemaking which other groups could use with the Peace Puzzle dove. This material was packaged in a vinyl case along with a television commercial and was distributed throughout the country.

The felt dove was a problem. How could we have these manufactured? Henk Bossers served a church of older people. He presented my problem to the Be Better Christians class. All the women in the class were more than eighty years old! They agreed to help us. Those dear folks cut out four hundred sets of felt doves for the peacemaking kits as their contribution to the study of peace.

It is important to note that the development of resources for being the visible church locally is often missed by many churches. Most local folks assume that a national headquarters or a publishing house will create the materials needed for ministry. I believe that if you can create something that helps people in your church or community to become more faithful to Jesus Christ, you have a responsibility to share it with others. This is not a matter of ego or status. The most authentic moments of the visible church's life develop at the local level.

Several hundred of these study kits were shared with churches around the country. The response from those using it indicated that it was blessing to people in very different settings.

MEDIA

We had developed the dove devotional program and group study material, and we now pushed into the mass media world. Five thirty-second spots were produced for $5,000. They began with six seconds of animation. Pieces of the Peace Puzzle dove moved from a random relationship to form the dove, designed to look like a stained-glass window. A children's choir recorded background music, using percussion instruments.

Then a fifteen-second vignette was featured before a repeat of the opening animation. Each spot dealt with a different problem: street crime, neighborhood anger, family difficulties, union-management problems, racial conflict.

For instance, following the opening animation, the spot dealing with union-management problems showed two men arm wrestling. One was dressed in office garb, while the other wore work clothes. We shot the spot on a playground, with the men on a hand-driven merry-go-round which was moved slowly while the men struggled. This gave the viewer the impression that the camera was moving around the men in constant struggle.

An announcer from a radio station read the voice-over narration, a news report about a management and union dispute which ended in the closing of the plant. The spot ended with question, "Could love provide another way?"

These spots were run as public-service announcements. They were also used in local churches for study and discussion groups. Thirty thousand people participated in these devotional exercises.

It would have been useful to utilize newspaper ads, bumper stickers, and other forms of display advertising, but we didn't use those additional opportunities. We ran out of time and money. The Peace Puzzle dove designed to look like stained-glass would have been excellent in display advertising. More ecumenical involvement would also been helpful.

The use of a phone system could provide audio devotional support in this model. A local church with a recorded phone system could record an exercise each day. A family could simply call the number and receive instructions and encouragement.

The computer could also be employed to gather the names of people in the network of devotional activity. Each member could be given the names and number of others. A computer system could be devised by which names would be exchanged so that each night one family would call another with a special blessing.

AND SO . . .

The Peace Puzzle is an exciting example of ways your church can reach many people with a controversial aspect of faith. The plan demonstrates some important aspects of the visible church's outreach.

1. Inclusiveness of people with different viewpoints is important, and possible, in dealing with issues that initially might seem divisive.

2. Inclusiveness of age groups is vital, and possible, in dealing with the intergenerational church. The whole family of God can worship and struggle together with important matters of faith.

3. Evangelism will be undertaken by those who are hesitant about reaching out to others, when they see it as a gift that will bless others.

4. Group media (the things a group does with media) is a fantastic basis for reaching out to others, and changing people with the gospel.

5. It is important, and possible, to be ecumenical as we reach for the deepest of faith concerns.

Shape this model of the visible church to serve the ministry of your church. You will find all kinds of new people of goodwill who seek a community of faith which cares about the travail of the world. You will be blessed by being peacemakers.

Chapter 7

THE PEOPLE TREE:
A MODEL FOR
STEWARDSHIP

"At the last moment of the church's life, there will be a sermon and an offering." Although the cynicism of the remark is off base, it is true that the need for financial resources to undertake ministry is always with us.

The Bible clearly acknowledges that in this world there must be resources to do the work of faith. The apostle Paul spent a good portion of his energies raising money for those in the church who faced poverty. The concept of the biblical tithe, a 10 percent gift off the top of one's income, is considered, even if briefly, by most serious Christians. There can be no visible church without a visible sign of support.

Yet, for the average Christian, money is also the cause of much confusion, shame, anger, and fear. Paul's warning about the love of money being the root of all evil appears to be the source of much Christian discomfort.

To receive interest from the lending of money was outlawed by church edict for several centuries, and the people of God were often driven to forsake material possessions. St. Francis shed his very clothes in his act of surrendering his former life to serve the church in poverty.

In spite of this struggle of conscience against the lust for money, it is obvious that throughout history, the Christian's quest for riches has not been slowed. In fact, many barons of industry in early and present America have wiggled past these shafts of doubt by seeing wealth as a blessing from God. They contend that if all things come from God, the Lord must be blessing them with money. In other words, God blessed the wealthy with wealth and the poor with poverty. This is a simple statement of a complex struggle concerning the theology of money and power. Unfortunately, it is the formula accepted by many contemporary Christians.

The continuous criticism in the American body politic concerning welfare and help for the needy stems from those understandings. For many, there is simply no place for helping those in poverty. If the poor were faithful and worked hard, God would have provided them with wealth.

The theological understanding about money is further confused by reports which periodically appear before the public concerning the misuse and abuse of money by religious people. It doesn't matter to the popular mind that the misuse of religious funds in a particular case came from a Lone Ranger religious leader. To the public, this example of inexcusable behavior taints the whole Church.

The billion-dollar-a-year religious media industry has taken a credibility bashing in the past few years. Some of those media stars have taken short cuts in the methods they use to raise personal funds. Money hasn't always gone to the causes earmarked by the donors, excessive sums have gone to luxury items for the leaders, and the cost of raising the money has seriously diminished the funds that reach those who deserve it.

There is no excuse for false appeals, misuse of funds, and other shady practices. However, many of these people have simply been trapped in the mass-media addiction. If one must come up with a million dollars a week to stay on the air, one will feel the pressure of cash-flow problems. Under stress, it can be tempting to employ questionable fund-raising tactics.

One "Peanuts" cartoon shows one of the characters sitting in front of a television set. The balloon over the set becomes more and more shrill with each panel. "If I don't get your money immediately, this will be my last program," it screams in the next to last panel. The character on the beanbag simply responds, "Bye."

Charles Schultz is a great cartoonist and a fine Christian. And he is expressing the real reaction of the public to most religious money appeals. Unfortunately, at this very time in history, the church needs financial resources more than ever if it is to take on the task of ministry before it. How far can the church go in asking for money? What means are consistent with our spiritual character? How can we convince our people of the need to support the ministry of the gospel through the local, national, and international body of Christ?

These questions are very important because all of us live in the material world. Many of our members have supported electronic preachers, although they too may now be turned off by those hucksters of TV religion. But all our people continue to make choices in every part of their lives, under the influence of this same kind of media persuasion. How do we reach people who have been raised on a new song in a strange land? How does the visible church convincingly present to people living in the visible world the financial needs of the ministry dictated by the invisible church?

"The story is the thing that will catch the conscience of the believer." Our apologies to Shakespeare. However, Tom Boomershine, my colleague at United Theological Seminary, is right when he lifts up the saving and healing aspects of the biblical story. We are Christians today because of the stories carried to us by our forebears in the faith. It was the telling of the saving acts of God around campfires, dinner tables, and hospital beds which enabled us to acknowledge the work God has completed and is doing in Jesus Christ.

There is more to telling the biblical story than merely saying the words. It is the Holy Spirit that enables the telling and hearing to take place in such a way that there is life change in the receiver.

A noted scholar suggested a series of biblical stories one must be able to tell to be a Christian. These stories start with the Garden of Eden. One must also be able to tell the story of one's particular religious heritage. However, the final story to be told by a Christian is the personal faith journey. He then suggests that the most important role of the church leader is to build a campfire, around which the people can tell their faith stories.

The telling of the faith story is an intimate and powerful experience. Testimonies have been one of the first and most enduring needs of the church. As time pushed the church further from those who had seen Jesus and the disciples in the flesh, there was more and more need for the witness of believers. The invisible faith became visible through the lives of those who lived in Christ and in whom Christ lived. There is comfort in getting close to your spiritual roots.

It is also a blessing to bear the story to others. The act of putting into words the experience of the way God has worked in your life enlivens the reality of the story. There is an intimacy between faith and my being when I share how Jesus is experienced in my life. The Word becoming sound—my sound—is incarnate in my words. I am inseparable from the story of salvation.

This strange and wondrous dynamic is not often considered in discussions of communication. Most often, media are viewed in terms of spacial concepts. The media product is out there. "If we can just get that awful rock star with the foul mouth off the stage, our children will be safe." The fact is, once the media experience has been experienced, it exists in a nonspacial dimension. The song lives on in the performer, in the individual listener, and in the media form (record, sound system, etc.). Each of the communication forms has a different meaning, a different impact, and a different reality.

I was a talk-show host on a rock station for more than seventeen years. Each week I spoke with people from a five-state area about some of the deepest human concerns. Unemployed miners, victims of AIDS, cocaine users and dealers, and people on the edge of suicide have shared their lives with me. These stories of desperation touched me and those who listened. Some people were changed in obvious ways, and most found the program a resting place where they could tell their stories to someone who cared. There was a strange and moving communion between the listeners and myself.

When I left the show to take a position at a seminary in another city, I experienced an unexpected depression. My storytelling intimacy with the listeners had an intensity quite different from face-to-face communication. The last show was very emotional. The callers and I wept openly. "I have talked with you for twenty years. I don't even know what you look like."

The first week in seventeen years that would not conclude with that show was very difficult. I told my colleagues at the seminary about my grief. With impish glee, one said that the first Sunday morning I wasn't on the air, he would call me with a personal problem.

I suggest that you can draw upon these insights, this special medium, and the relationship of the faith stories in building a special stewardship campaign.

GOALS

The program would pursue the following goals:

1. Collect the stories of faith from every member of the congregation.
2. Focus the spiritual legacy of the church through its people.
3. Conduct a stewardship campaign that would bring the strongest response in the history of the church.

THE PLAN

This campaign is built around the simple premise that people will support the church both finanacially and otherwise, when it is clear that it is an extension of their faith. It is my hunch that this basic truth is best experienced when an individual is able to offer his or her story to the community of Christ.

I also believe that an interview with an audio-cassette recorder is the mode of faith storytelling that makes the most impact on the teller. This assumption is based on two factors. First, the use of an electronic media form adds the quality of permanence. The recorded story has been preserved and transformed, and the person being interviewed knows that the story will be heard by others. During ordinary conversation, one is never sure whether one is being heard or not.

Second, the story told in the presence of a sensitive interviewer, a microphone, and a recorder, transports the interviewee into a different status. He or she is now a media maker—Mother Teresa, Johnny Carson, Bruce Springfield, or Dolly Parton. Media involvement lifts the encounter to a special level. Through the audio interview, the ordinary person becomes extraordinary.

I remember a visit to a nursing home. When I was shown to the person I was to visit, she was staring into space without any sign of vitality. When I introduced myself, she barely stirred. But when I brought out the microphone and invited her to tell her story, a strange transformation took place in that elderly woman. Her eyes focused, her chin lifted, her back straightened, and her hands leaped into the air with animation. Her story was inseparable from her life.

ORGANIZATION

I suggest that you organize a team of youth and adults. Ask them to take on a six-to-eight-month task. Take them through the process of interviewing with cassette tape recorders. They will then visit and interview every member of the church! One of the team members will take several slides or pictures of each interviewee.

"I never told anyone this . . ." I have heard this phrase many times during the past twenty-one years. In the course of my interviewing experience I have spoken with thousands of people for radio and television. They have given the most intimate accounts of their hopes, dreams, failures, and faith.

"I feel as if I have been in a confessional . . ." The rock star didn't know his interviewer was a clergyperson. He just knew that the process of telling his story in the presence of a microphone had changed his feelings and his life. In the hands of a Christian, the microphone becomes a means of grace.

At every possible opportunity, I teach people how to utilize this most accessible of modern mediums. Over the past two decades, workshop participants have been pushed out into the world with microphone in hand.

THE EQUIPMENT

Audio-cassette machines are everywhere. They can be purchased reasonably or borrowed from almost anyone. Do not use the machines with built-in microphones. They pick up not only the sound you want, they pick up *all* sounds.

You will need an extension microphone. You might be able to borrow the mike used in your sanctuary. Then find a conversion plug so that the mike can be connected to your recorder. If you have to buy an extension mike, spend $15 or more. Don't buy a $3 wonder.

You will need a recorder that costs $50 or more. It is also

important that you use good quality cassettes. The very cheap tapes are poor quality or reworked computer tape, which is hard on your recording heads. Quality tapes can be purchased inexpensively from wholesale companies in lots of twenty-five or more. They usually can be obtained for eighty cents or so in lots of one hundred. Every resource closet should have that many good quality cassettes on hand.

You may want to clean the recording and playback heads on the inside of the recorder. These are found in the area where the edge of the tape meets the machine. Residue builds up on these areas, and if you don't clean them, the sound will become diminished.

THE INTERVIEW

It is important to be present when receiving the faith story of another person. He or she will "read" your face, the language of your body, the compassion and understanding in your eyes. The interviewer communicates more loudly by presence than by words.

To get good quality sound recording, the mike must be held carefully so that the sound of handling it won't disturb the sound of the voices. It should be close to the mouth of the interviewee, but to one side. If it is directly in front of the lips, some people will expel air and create "pops."

It is the good and empathetic listener who will get the story. These are very special people of faith who are giving you their greatest and most treasured possession—their lives. This is not an exercise in quest of debate, or counseling, or conversation. Your interviewing team is called to be the ear of God on behalf of the faith community.

There are three steps to most interviews. *The contract* will have been established through communications in the newsletter, the weekly bulletins, and from the pulpit. However, each time you visit someone for the story, it is vital that you inform the person about what you are doing (getting the story), why you are doing it (to gather the faith story of the church), and how you are going to use it (to share with the congregation an oral history, and for the stewardship dinner).

The second step in a good interview is *the encounter* itself.

This is the time of listening and feeling with the storyteller. A good interviewer listens carefully to pick up all the verbal and nonverbal clues for the full story. It is best to ask questions that can't be answered incorrectly. For instance, one would not ask interviewees to criticize the minister. But they might be asked what they would do if they were pastor.

The third step is *the conclusion*. It is important that the interviewers thank the people and confirm that it was important that their story be shared. Sometimes I have even played a bit of the interview back to people who have never heard their own voices.

For the sake of getting the faith history of your church for the stewardship program, I will suggest three beginning questions, or areas, of faith sharing. The first could be, "If you were God looking at our church, what particular thing would make you happiest?" Your interviewees aren't God, but they can comfortably begin their story of faith through the church by taking this perspective. Then move the person toward more personal, specific examples.

The second question could be, "If you were God looking at our church, what particular things would you want us to do that we haven't done?" This will lead the person to suggest new directions for the church.

The third could be, "If you were God looking at our church, what particular things do you think should be changed?" This may lead to parts of the story that might be critical.

Of course, these are only beginning points for the faith story. The more personal the stories are, the more important they will be. People will open doors in their comments and invite you in. The interviewer needs to listen carefully in order to pick up those clues and enter those doors.

Your folks will be very open in their willingness to help with these interviews. They may want to talk immediately about how personal lives have been changed by God through your church. You will still want them to be specific.

This listening experience will take time. Yet the very process of hearing the stories of a whole congregation will bring an amazing transformation to the church. For the first time, people will have a chance to be heard.

It is a sad realization that most churches operate on a

pathological communication mode. People receive attention only if they are upset about something, experience a tragedy, or have a personal problem. Those who are generally happy or do not communicate their concerns receive no attention. Their one visit may be in connection with the stewardship drive.

This model is very different. Wonderful stories will surface in the course of the interviews. There will be a sense of acceptance, care, and hope in this campaign to collect the faith experiences of the faith community.

AFTER THE VISITS

The team will next need to organize the interviews so that selected portions can be lifted out. These will be used at the congregational banquet, a stewardship dinner that will be a celebration of the faith story of the church.

Others will plan the dinner and advertise it, and it is important to do this well. Focus the publicity on the People Tree. Announce that stories from the interviews will be shared.

Organize the room for the dinner by positioning several projection screens on opposing walls. Slide projectors can be placed in the center. This will permit you to show several slides at one time and will flood the congregation with pictures and voices from many different people in a short time.

On the night of the stewardship dinner, build upon the theme of The People Tree. The term *tree* is used also in the Bible to describe the Cross. If you have some folks with artistic skills, this connection might be a good clue. Many of the stories will reveal that the people in your church are bearing their crosses through their ministry with others.

Your decoration/publicity task force can decorate the room, print the programs, and make name tags with the People Tree motif. By the way, don't overlook the importance of name tags. Even in small churches, some people don't know the name of every single person. The evening can move in four or five parts. The interviewing team will put together a terse collection of segments from the interviews, with accompanying slides. They might want to follow the basic questions as they were asked. The segments should not be longer than four or five minutes. After each portion, encourage the tables of people to continue by telling their stories to one another. In a few minutes, continue with the next segment.

You might want to develop a pledge form in the shape of a people tree. Each story shared at the table can be logged in during the discussion. At the bottom, people can write in their own story.

After an hour or so they all will catch the message: *They* are the body of Christ. It is their faith story that provides the ministry of the church. The theme of the People Tree can be contrasted to the common family tree.

The People Tree pledge form can be explained at this time.

MEDIA

A computer hack in your congregation can add a number of touches to this program. He or she may want to have your interviewers do some data collecting while the interviews are being undertaken. A whole talent bank could be developed. Imagine how your educational program could be enriched if you could retrieve the names of people who had been to camp as children!

Or if you had the names of everyone who has moved out of town or is away at school or in the service, you could add connections to the family tree. Imagine how much the outreach of the church could be strengthened by an intentional pattern of writing to those who are away. The local church has been negligent in serving those who are not present but still are part of the community. Many young people feel deserted by the faith community when they go away to work, to study, or to serve their country.

The computer is not a cold, mechanical technology. It can be a means by which the gospel is communicated to others.

AND SO . . .

This stewardship program can be one of the most successful you have ever had. It will open new avenues of creativity and sharing in the congregation. There will be a bonding between the ministry of the church and the members of the faith community. The people of God will always support that which they believe is inspired and which they fully understand to be part of their own ministry.

This model underscores a few clues about the visible church:

1. Money is not a shameful resource, an impossible goal, or an unfit concern for spiritual people.

2. The interlocking connection between the personal faith story and the proclamation of the gospel will trigger generosity.

3. The church's media outreach is most authentic when it focuses on the stories of believers, not those of egocentric stars.

4. Each church contains a reservoir of compelling faith stories that are never heard in the course of the usual church programming.

Chapter 8

THE FEAST OF FOOLS:
A MODEL FOR FALL
OUTREACH

"I never did this before." The elderly man paused. Then he brushed paste on the back of a piece of paper and confidently placed the picture he had torn from the magazine on the refrigerator box. He smiled as he surveyed the huge cross that he, a teenaged girl, a toddler, three middle-aged people, and four young adults had created. They were participating in an amazing model for the visible church—The Feast of Fools.

Ed McNulty is one of the most creative Christians I know. He is a former classmate, my former pastor, and a long-time friend. I have experienced Ed's delightful creation The Feast of Fools on several occasions, and it has been a real blessing to all who participated in it.

Ed was reading Harvey Cox's book *Feast of Fools* and was struck by the concept drawn from the Middle Ages celebration, Feast of Fools. The world was turned upside down during that special festival. Lords became lowly fools and simple fools became rulers—at least, for one day, the people transformed their appearances and public behavior in such an inversion, Donning costumes, they celebrated with games, skits, and food.

Paul's idea of being a fool for Christ came to Ed's mind. How could the local church draw upon Paul's concept? Why couldn't that ancient secular celebration become useful in helping the local church reach out? They could touch the community with celebration, imagination, and prophetic imagery.

He decided to use the Halloween celebration in the American culture as the time for this community-wide event.

GOALS

Three goals emerged from this model for the visible church:

1. To provide an experience for an intergenerational, intercultural, and interclass group to experience the inclusive community created by Christ.
2. To provide an opportunity for an inclusive community to share their creativity.
3. To provide an opportunity for the continuity of faith from the past to be experienced in the present.

Ed was well aware of the problems and confusion that have emerged around Halloween in some communities. Some Christian groups have publicly worried about the cultic images that appear in some costumes and celebrations during that season. Other Christians have been upset because some children around the world who receive food and milk bought with the money donated in the local UNICEF drives may be communist.

These problems present many implications concerning one's theology. However, Ed's model is one of positive transformation and has received support from an amazing cross-section of people. I think you will find broad acceptance of this model in most communities.

THE PLAN

The Feast of Fools is a special gift for the people in the church. They are given an opportunity to invite their friends to an occasion when imagination and joy transform moments of play into a celebration of the love of Christ.

The participants are encouraged to wear costumes which transform their ordinary selves into an opposite person. They may want to focus on great people from the church's past. Gather some old clothes and masks as the makings for costumes for those who may be hesitant about dressing for the occasion.

Your folks will be involved in a movable feast during which the foolishness of the gospel will be enjoyed. The two or three hours of fun and activity will conclude with a special worship experience.

MEDIA

This will also be a major outreach into the community. The media will be excited about this unusual event offered by a local church. It will provide an excellent way to interpret the nature and history of the Christian community.

Encourage any artists in your church to develop a striking logo. For instance, they could design a clown with small crosses on its face.

You must seek people who ordinarily don't visit your church. Remember that you are turning things upside down. For instance, visit the retirement homes and arrange to transport those folks to your feast! Don't underestimate the elders of the tribe. They will love this kind of celebration.

Numerous people are on the brink of coming to church, but they need a nudge to experience the love of Christ before they can make a commitment. How can you reach the apartment dwellers, trailer-park inhabitants, condo owners? Perhaps you can use direct mail (every-household mailings).

The youth can campaign at school for this party. They make the most impact by simply bringing friends. There are so many young people longing for the fellowship of the church.

Use display advertising. Posters in stores and huge banners across the church lawn will raise community awareness of the ministry of the church.

Have your people write invitations to friends and relatives. You can supply the notes and envelopes during a worship service, and the invitations can be collected after the service and mailed. It is important that your members understand the importance of such a visible manifestation of the faith community. Perhaps a series of sermons about Paul's image of being fools for Christ could provide the foundation for this preparation.

Remember the need for multiple impressions to make impact on your people and those around you in the community. Once the event is successfully undertaken, your members will look forward to its appearance next year, and other moments of reaching out.

ORGANIZATION

This model demands the use of most of your church, or at least many rooms and large open spaces. It is amazing how the dull

space of a church basement can be transformed with imagination
and hard work. Just remember what you used to do in that high
school gym for those special occasions. You have wonderfully
creative people in your church. Once they see a dream, they will
exceed all your expectations.

Imagine a medieval marketplace. There need to be many
stalls, activity centers, eating places, and space for a closing
worship experience. There is no limit to the setting you can
create in your church.

THE STALLS

At Paste Place there will be makings for collage construction.
Here people can decorate a large cross. You will need several
large boxes, which can be found at appliance stores. You will
need to decide how they can be joined together to form a cross
after people have covered them with pictures and words from
magazines, crayon drawings, and other creative designs.

The Apple Dunk is another interest center. Apples can be
floated in a large barrow or tub filled with water. Participants will
dunk their faces in the water to try to bite into an apple and hold
on to it. You will need paper towels to dry the faces of those
dunking.

In Celebration Place, participants will develop the creative
worship service that will end the evening. An enabler will be
there to help them prepare. You may want to use the clown
worship service format for this group, following the outline of
your regular worship service. Assist the teams of participants as
they work on different parts of the service. Encourage them to
enable the group to experience that part of the liturgy. If you are
a clown, you can lead the congregation of fools through the use of
mime.

The sermon will be in the form of a slide and sound
presentation on the fools for Christ throughout the centuries.
Pictures of Sarah, Calvin, Luther, Wesley, St. Francis, Mother
Teresa, Martin Luther King, and others can be copied from
magazines and other publications by a photographer in the
congregation. Have the people in the Celebration Place write
the script. How were the "fools for Christ" really fools?

Or you might write the script ahead of time. Ed followed the latter course. Whichever path you take, you will want the script read aloud while the slides are shown.

The Harvest Shed focuses on crafts made from natural items. During fall in most parts of the country, special products of nature will be available—corn husks, gourds, dried flowers, seeds, and so on. Someone in your community or church should be able to provide expertise in this area. Ed utilized the skills of a person in the congregation who was an expert in early American crafts. She led the group in making dolls from corn husks.

You might want the center to focus on creating table centerpieces for Thanksgiving. These can be given away to retirement homes or to the homebound. A centerpiece for the Communion table or altar would be a terrific project for your church.

The Shaving Place features whittling. Again, there should be someone in the community or church who does woodworking, and he or she can set up a process by which young and old can make beautiful things. It is amazing what can be created out of scraps of wood, under the tutelage of a good woodworker. For instance, an older man in one congregation worked with teenagers on a project. They made beautiful crosses by using sandpaper and simple tools.

The Paper Crease utilizes the art of paper folding. Origami, a Japanese art form, is excellent for this booth. Beautiful birds, fish, flowers, and other breathtaking creations can be made by folding paper. There are great folks who can teach this to those at The Feast of Fools. In the past couple of years, many church groups have been using origami to make cranes to commemorate the atomic bombing of Hiroshima. Imagine paper creations that could be used as decorations for Christmas trees!

The Harp Haven is a musical activity center which focuses on participatory music. You will need a resource person who can help the participants write a hymn or song for the worship service. The person should be the kind who can take the words, images, and ideas of the participants as the makings for a song and can then set it to music. The group can work at performing the hymn in all kinds of different styles. They will lead the folks in singing their hymn during the worship service.

The Body Shop is the place where a couple of local artists can paint designs on the faces, hands, or arms of the participants. Have them develop two or three Christian designs which communicate the love and joy of the gospel. Children will particularly love this center.

You can see the kind of activity Ed's design encourages. Your folks have been conducting vacation church schools and designing church bazaars, so they have many fantastic ideas for such booths. You can probably design a dozen other centers. It is important that the results of these activities be shared at the worship service. A sharing time or a giving of gifts can permit each person to make an offering before God.

Refreshments

Food is an important part of a feast. Churches have traditionally been the source of special food in the context of wonderful hospitality. The Feast of Fools is the time to roll out great fun food. Ed tries to utilize food that gives the feel of the Middle Ages. One year he featured chicken drumsticks, corn on the cob, and fresh fruit, all served in bowls. No utensils were needed. A special punch was served hot. This "mead" was made of fruit juice and lots of spices. It had a taste most people had not experienced previously. There were many eating places, and people were encouraged to eat as they worked.

Worship Event

The worship event closes out the experience. It will be a vigorous and happy time, with all the people participating and sharing their gifts.

Afterward, gather your planning committee and evaluate the event. What stories of special moments unfolded during the evening? What was the high point? How many came? What could have been done differently?

Make plans right now for the next year. The longer you can look forward to this new annual event, the better you can prepare for it.

AND SO . . .

Ed gives us a special model for the visible church. The basic outline can be modified and expanded at any point as you make it your own. There are several special contributions The Feast of Fools offers your church:

1. It transforms a secularized community holiday into a special Christian experience.

2. It provides an experiential opportunity through which people can learn about their forebears in the faith who have risked to be fools for Christ.

3. It raises the awareness in the community of the church's vitality and creativity.

4. It offers the congregation a specific occasion when they can invite others to the church. They will be proud to have others share something special.

5. It gives the stranger a special setting in which inclusiveness and hospitality can be experienced.

6. It provides a time when all generations can celebrate God's joyful love as a total community.

7. It takes very few financial resources to plan and execute.

Don't overlook this model as you plan to become the visible church in your community.

Chapter 9

FREE THE HOSTAGES: A MODEL FOR POLITICAL CHANGE

"I want to be on your show and talk about the military build-up."

"Do you know who the audience is?"

"No. I want to tell your listeners the facts about government spending on the military."

"Our audience is composed of males age eighteen to thirty-five, who love Rambo films and want to kill commies. How do you expect to reach them?"

This kind of dialogue took place at least twice a week during the past twenty years as folks sought to be guests on my radio talk show. Such people are on the cutting edge of social change. In striving for justice, they often have this kind of media difficulty.

They focus so intensely on their issue that they are unable or unwilling to seriously consider the context, the receiver of the message, or the medium being used. Whether their appearance will make any difference in the lives of the receivers seems to be unimportant to them. There is apparent satisfaction in merely saying their truth.

It is strange that many folks concerned about change in our culture have not realized that there are ways that mass media will cooperate with them and their issues. A broadcaster is most concerned about whether a guest or a message will be interesting and good entertainment. Radio and television are really designed to entertain.

The fact that some wish they were educational, in the sense that a classroom used to be educational, is beside the point. We watch or listen in order to be distracted, pleased, fascinated, or sometimes challenged.

There is no reason our messages can't be compelling and interesting. Jesus certainly was an engaging communicator. We must be willing to explore every communication form in our quest for means to present the gospel in a more creative way. Many Christians are blinded by the secular or alien context of communication innovation. They cannot separate the form from the context.

For instance, most electronic evangelists are exciting and intriguing presenters. I may argue with their messages, but I must admit they offer good media form.

How do we combine life-giving messages with powerful forms that will be appreciated and willingly used by mass media? This is the challenge that faces Christians who want to make their faith touch the lives of others in matters of social transformation.

THE PLAN

We stumbled into the American hostage situation by accident. Carol Weir had just begun her public crusade to win the freedom of her husband and the other six Americans being held in Lebanon. We had read a notice about her visit to Pittsburgh, where she appeared at a local church for a meeting of twenty or thirty people. The papers barely mentioned her visit.

I rode in the car that took her to the airport and interviewed her in the airport parking lot. Gregg Hartung and I then mixed these voice tracks from Carol and her son, John, with music and the voice of an announcer.

In New York, Carol had been told that there was no money for media support, but I called the church official there and played the spots we had crafted. I told him I was pretty sure that many stations would carry them. "I can have them to the tape duplicator immediately, and he will mail them to every station in the country within three days. It will cost $13,000."

He paused for about thirty seconds before he answered. "Go ahead. I will have the money to you immediately."

The spots were designed to appeal to American patriotism and sympathy for the wife of a hostage. They ended with the announcer asking listeners to write to the President.

A cover letter from a church official was included in each package with the reel-to-reel copy of the spots. We also asked the stations to fill out a card with their schedule for playing the spots.

The response was fantastic. Over a thousand stations carried the messages, averaging five times a week for ninety days. We figured we received more than $1,000,000 worth of air time. Many of the reply cards promised that the spots would be run until the hostages were released.

The denomination had hoped that the President would receive a million letters about the hostages. The White House never released the number of letters received from the campaign, but we do know that several new secretaries were hired to handle the increased mail.

We next developed a series of ten-second television spots with Steve Allen. The Presbyterian Church and Catholic Relief Services cooperated in paying for these, which were carried by two hundred stations. Since we designed them to be used when there were different numbers of hostages, some stations were running them two years later!

Many things were done on behalf of the hostages by many people, and the use of mass media was important. After Ben Weir was released we decided that a book would keep the issue alive in another way. *Hostage Bound, Hostage Free* drew more interest from print and electric media—Ben was able to talk about the hostages who were still in captivity.

This model will also work for the local churches that are concerned about local issues.

MEDIA

Newspapers are a particularly important outlet. Yet most people do not use this source properly. They may buy an ad on the religious page to announce the Sunday services or send a release to promote an activity. The former isn't likely to reach the unchurched, and the latter does not merit a significant news story.

Newspapers too are designed to please and entertain the reader. Publishers are not against stories about faith and religion, but the stories must be newsworthy.

For instance, if you reached out to the community through an ice-cream social, the usual approach would be to write an announcement with information about the event. This is not news. It is only an attempt to get a free ad.

The local newspaper would treat the story differently if you sent along the newsworthy essence of the event—people. What if you mentioned that an eighty-five-year-old woman had been attending the event for the past seventy years? Her grandmother was a slave. She has seen history unfold during her lifetime. The papers would be interested in doing a feature about this intriguing person. Of course, somewhere in the article they would mention that she would be attending your ice-cream social.

I have found that once reporters discover that you are a source of good stories, you will be called for leads. In fact, I developed a file of people from the faith community who had something important to tell, and I would give the reporters those names.

Each time your church has a story in the body of the newspaper (not on the religion page), more people are touched with the gospel. Stories are the heart of good reporting. Remember that you are custodian of an endless reservoir of stories. You have an intimate relationship with the most extraordinary people in the culture. They have the rare ability to see God's work in the ordinary. The Christian faith is a witnessing life. Where else can we find people who are near death, face unemployment, fight abuse, or confront prejudice, and still can offer hope and love to others?

The Press Conference

The media will gather to hear stories that are news. The press conference is an excellent way to get wide coverage for activities that touch a number of different people. When Carol and Ben Weir were in Dayton, Ohio, for the taping of a video study course, I conducted a press conference. Let's review the series of steps in planning such an event:

1. Arrange for a room large enough to accomodate newspaper, radio, and television reporters. I even had lights from our video studio set up to provide more light for the television cameras.

2. Send a release to each of the media people with emphasis on the news aspects of your announcement. In the case of Ben Weir—former hostage and then current moderator of the

Presbyterian Church—a conversation with the recently released hostage Father Martin was real news.

3. Call each media outlet both the day before the conference and on the day of the conference.

4. Arrange to have the conference early enough so that the media people can make the deadlines for that day.

5. Set up the room so that the name of the sponsors (in our case, the seminary.) could be in most of the television shots.

6. Invite the highest local official of the church to the conference.

7. Give the presiding official a brief statement to be read at the opening of the conference.

8. Distribute copies of another press release at the conference.

9. Focus on the most immediate national news story which would tie into your conference, giving a context for the coverage. (Another hostage had been taken the day we had our conference.)

I closed the conference with a reminder that Dr. Weir was the only former hostage giving interviews on the day another hostage had been taken and that the networks would be interested in television footage.

Attendance was excellent and the coverage was superb. All three networks took the feeds from their affiliates. We made both evening and morning news across the country!

It is often important to open a press conference with a carefully prepared statement by the person being interviewed, but it must be written with the needs of the media in mind.

A friend of mine called a press conference years ago in Chicago. He had just put together an amazing coalition of churches to combat a major community problem, and he proudly read his carefully prepared ten-minute statement at the beginning of the press conference. As the crews were putting away their equipment, a cameraman told my friend how much he appreciated this opening statement. "It's too bad we won't be using it." My friend asked why it would not be used.

The man answered, "It was so carefully prepared we can't edit it. We need only tight ten-second bites. Sorry."

AND SO . . .

You may think this model is beyond your immediate need or interest. However, any speaker or visitor can provide the kind of news that would interest local media. Our faith demands that we work to change many conditions in the world. It might be a school issue, local hunger, unemployment, the need for a hospice, the treatment of street people, almost anything. Think in terms of bringing such a condition before people as a newsworthy item.

This model provides the flow you need in order to utilize the local media in the attempt to reach out in the name of the gospel to affect the world around you.

You may find that you can use this model to help others in their ministry of caring. The role of chaplaincy to others who are deeply involved in social change is vital

Many folks have the right instinct, but for the wrong reasons. As Christians, we know that God has sent Jesus Christ in order that all of life may be touched.

We also know that it is not our efforts that will bring the kingdom of God. We do not reach out to bring the gospel to social institutions in order to please ourselves. We participate in such incarnational ministry simply to be faithful to Christ.

Chapter 10

THE RALLY: A MODEL FOR SUNDAY SCHOOL OUTREACH

"Our church used to have more people in Sunday school than at Sunday worship. Now we don't even have a Sunday school!" That older man is clearly worried about this radical change in his local church. He knows the change is due to many complex shifts in the times and in the population. There is something strange and frightening going on in the educational life of the Christian church.

The visible church can be only a reflection of what is really happening in the life of the local church. We can't make visible that which is not true, available, or happening. Such a stance makes it difficult for the committed person to utilize media opportunities. How do we begin the process of reaching out when there is little to share? This is the nightmare faced by those who want to bring Christ to the world. Any church can be filled at any given time, but if the Spirit of God is not experienced, visitors will not come back again.

This tension between what is and what could be is the starting place for those who seek a renewed ministry. The cycle between being lively, and communicating that liveliness to others, is not solved by following a linear pattern. A church can't wait to get its Sunday school at full strength before sharing this reality with others. It is also impossible to mount an outreach program unless the church is poised for ministry.

The Rally is nothing more than an all-out effort to make people aware of the opening day of Church school. The model includes programming the church to teach and inviting the people to come—using all the media resources at hand!

The gentleman who is worried about the extinction of his church's Sunday school knows that something is wrong. How can he help to turn it around? This model will suggest one way this can be approached.

GOALS

The goals for The Rally:

1. To focus the energy of the local church on the Sunday school.
2. To prepare a place where young and old, members and strangers, will feel the hospitality of Christ.
3. To raise the awareness in the community to the vitality and faithfulness of Christian education in the local church.
4. To gather the largest class of student in history for a Sunday school opening.

THE PLAN

We live in an area where there are churches with strong Sunday school classes and others with none at all. The education leaders have built an incredible annual event to train Sunday school teachers, an annual event which brings together the attributes of education and evangelism. "Evaneducation" is a fall gathering of eight hundred people who participate in a fantastic variety of workshops. And the energy and excitement has spilled out to all the local church programs.

This process for the regeneration of the Sunday school has been put in place by the West Ohio Conference of The United Methodist Church. The support of a regional group is often important to the renewal of educational programs in the local congregation. At least it is vital for awakening a sleepy situation.

The dynamic which sparks renewal in education is built around prayerful reflection on the needs that face the community of Christ. The educational workshop is one of the truly important aspects of finding direction for our prayers as educators. It is not the leadership or the information shared in these gatherings that is most important. I have led almost fifteen hundred such meetings over the past twenty years, and I am continually amazed by the way the Spirit of God works in these events. Each person receives a sense of being part of the struggling, suffering, rejoicing, giving body of Christ. The sum is so much greater than the parts we contribute. These renewal events are bathed in tears, laughter, sighs, and dreams. We experience the reality that ministry is demanding, and we learn from fellowship with others that it is possible to be faithful in any context.

If you are in a situation without denominational or regional support for the renewal of your Sunday school, a number of options still are open to you. You might hire a good workshop leader who can create a climate in which spiritual power and sharing can grow. Your denomination or other educators can recommend the names of such consultants.

Many churches have found that the best way to change the direction of their Sunday schools is to invest in their teachers. There are many fine workshops and continuing-education opportunities to which teachers can be sent. When the church chooses someone for special training, that person knows that he or she is doing something important.

ORGANIZATION

"Caverns of neglect." The noted educator shook his head. He has just returned from a six-month tour of Sunday schools across the country. He told me about the drab basements, the empty classrooms. "At one place, I stepped into a classroom and found two little girls sitting at a huge table. There were no decorations in the room, no sign of any activity. When I asked about their teacher, they said she just hadn't shown up."

Your church probably is not in such a state of neglect. However, it is important that the setting be right when others are invited for a visit. If the people who attend a rally catch the Spirit of God in your classes, they will continue to come and learn about the gospel for their lives.

The visible church is really the saints gathered around the gospel. Those who visit are able to see Christ as they experience the visible community. Yet, the people in many local churches find it difficult to be the incarnate kin of Christ. In fact, many adults are not comfortable with children and young people in the life of the church. They don't want the children in the worship service or the teens active in the power structure of the congregation. In fact, I saw one worship bulletin which stated that all children were to be removed from the sanctuary when the pastor began the sermon.

If this kind of attitude is present in your congregation, you will need to prepare the people for the big Sunday-school drive. Visitors will never return if there is this "closed circle" feeling in the congregation.

The matter of spiritual preparation for your church should begin with the committee in charge of the Sunday school. Through serious reflection, prayer, and a sense of imagination, this planning group can help the congregation create a climate of Christian hospitality.

It will be helpful to prepare a series of devotional studies for members of the congregation and the teaching staff; passages from the Old and New Testaments can provide the basis for religious education. There could be a series of sermons on this wonderful tradition of passing the faith on to others. It is the biblical foundation for the community that will create the right climate for the strangers.

COMPUTER

When the churches of a large area join together in this plan, the computer is a real help in working with lists of Sunday school teachers, pastors, and other members. To prepare them for the rally, personal letters can be sent in a series of steps, perhaps four or five letters over the course of several weeks. In fact, the computer and the data collected might be used to write to the children on the church rolls and in the community. This letter campaign can be most helpful in bringing the message of the rally to more people.

THE BUILDING

Perhaps your church isn't a "cavern of neglect," but you do need to look at the setting for The Rally. Drive up to your church and look at everything as if you were a visitor. Would you know where to enter? Could you easily find the proper classroom? What kind of feeling do you get when you look at the rooms for the classes? What kind of learning will take place in these spaces?

When the members of one church took this kind overview, they were amazed to learn that new people couldn't possibly find the right entrance. Several doors which were no longer used were permanently locked. Once inside, they found that the halls were dark, and successive building additions had made the journey to the sanctuary a minor expedition which only experienced guides could lead.

But they found an interesting solution to this negative presentation. The children and teachers painted big green footprints from the parking lot to the entrance. Inside, footprints were on the walls of the hallway that led to the classrooms! These decorative and funny designs were a bright and colorful solution.

The classrooms need a sense of visible warmth, excitement, and creativity. The room is the envelope in which the gospel will be presented, and it should show the spirit of its content. Public-school teachers, window dressers for department stores, or a local person involved in stage design can help you change the environment.

I have found that a basement setting can be transformed by billboard posters. Outdoor advertising companies can supply these huge sheets of paper. They are easy to put up and fantastic to look at.

MEDIA

We know what Sunday school is. We know that the learning experience enables others to grow in their understanding of Jesus Christ. However, it is easy for those in the church to look at those outside the church in a condescending manner: "We have the truth and you need to come to us to be as good as we are." It is easy to see why others in the community are not excited about coming to us. In fact, "Sunday school" is the topic of jokes in our day.

The Christian knows that the outside community has a mistaken view of the church and its ministry. We know that we are sinners in need of God's grace and that we embrace one another because of our need. We also know that God comes to us through our neighbors. In fact, we need the strangers, the babes in Christ, in order that we might grow in our understanding of

the way God works. We embrace new people in order to claim
the truth that they bring to us.

How can we include some of these thoughts in the message we
send out into the community? Probe for a phrase or slogan that
captures some of these themes. The armed forces have had great
success with the theme "Be all you can be." Perhaps you will
want to build on the message of stretching, challenge,
community, risking.

But watch for any indication of elitism or judgment that may
creep into your message. You are not doing strangers a favor by
inviting them to the event. This ministry is undertaken so that
you can be faithful to Christ. You have no option.

It is important to design the external part of the visible church
carefully. There is much available, so don't think small about
beckoning others to join you. Remember our principle of
multiple impressions: You must strive to create a holistic
message that will touch people several times in different ways.
The task of raising awareness demands intentionality, persistence, and patience.

This reach into the world should not be seen as merely a means
of bringing people to one Sunday event. In fact, I am not certain
that this plan will directly bring strangers into the church. The
best method is a personal invitation, but many of our people do
not have a strong appreciation of their own church—they are a
bit ashamed to invite friends.

It is the overall awareness of the church's ministry in the
community that will be raised by this outreach and result in
long-term benefits. Seeing their church in the mass media will
strengthen your members' pride and help them do the work of
outreach with more vigor.

Display

A banner is a good way to inform the community of your
special celebration. Some towns will permit churches and other
organizations to hang banners across the roads and highways.

It is important to think of perspective when designing roadside
signs to advertise activities. Two common mistakes can be made.
Most signs are too small and can't be seen from a car traveling
along the road. The letters must be large. Second, the paint on
most signs is not dark enough. Lightly lettered signs simply do

not make an impact. Have an experienced sign painter or artist do the job. Design is important.

Single billboards can be rented, and it may be possible to rent one or two in your town.

If you focus on a logo, you may want to use it in many different ways. For instance, bumper stickers are still the best way to raise awareness. Just a few will give the people in a community the impression that they have seen the stickers many different times.

How far do you want to go in your visible communication to gather young people and adults for this opening Sunday school event? Some churches have used attendance pins, McDonald's food certificates, prizes, and other means to persuade students to bring others.

These ideas may seem too worldly, but those who reach out to others in these ways feel that any means is justified in order to bring the stranger to the teaching situation. They know that once a person comes to a class, he or she will meet Jesus Christ. You will have to decide how far you want to go.

Television

If you have a budget and can undertake this program in cooperative with other churches, you may want to produce some television spots. Quality television material costs a great deal, yet some churches have been able to create video materials very inexpensively. One pastor paid a local cable station $300 to produce a simple spot. By using a football field and the athletic metaphor, the church found that the spot could be placed on the sports channel during big sports events at very little cost.

News coverage is one of your best possibilities. Sundays are usually low days for news stories. On Sunday evenings news stories are usually reduced to fires, auto accidents, and weather. A station would be delighted to have an interesting local story. Prepare the way by organizing interviews and classes with children to be photographed, and print releases that can be used by the reporters.

Newspapers

You probably will feel most comfortable with newspapers. Your church may currently buy space weekly to announce the worship services, but it is best to get stories into parts of the paper other than the religious page, if you want to reach people who are not currently related to the church. Refer to the advice in the last chapter. It is vital that you give the papers a story, not just a promotional announcement. They are looking for material that will interest readers, so look for that edge in this event.

For instance, you could build in a Sunday school reunion as part of Rally Day and ask people to wear the same clothes they wore during their childhood when they came to Sunday school.

The paper would be interested in the fact that people would gather from all around the country. Feed them some of the stories. Give them phone numbers of the people so that reporters can call for interviews. If you happen to have a famous person who attended years ago, that person could be used in the ads.

Radio

Radio stations are very sensitive to the audiences they serve. The stations will help you target the people you want to reach. For instance, if you are buying spots to reach young people, you might produce a spot that moves to the rhythms and language patterns of that audience. For adults, you would need to use a different approach on a different station.

Program directors are usually helpful to people who turn to them for advice in designing radio plans. These people have their fingers on the pulse of the listeners. They will also deal with the cost of buying time. Bargain for good rates.

Afterward

You will get one of the best turnouts in the life of your church if you undertake this plan with churchwide participation. Although one successful event is not a complete Christian-education program, this experience will do much to change the attitude of many concerning the church.

A number of questions face your church now. Have you affirmed the teachers, children, and others for their help in making the program a success? How do you get the students back the next Sunday? and the next? Did the strangers come again and become part of the community of faith? How can the parents be involved in the life of the church? How will the church be changed by the infusion of these new folks? The answers to these questions are really the basis for evaluating your success in using this model.

The expansion of the Sunday school can quicken the life of the whole church. Children can be the instruments of spiritual development.

AND SO . . .

The teaching of the depth, continuity, and complexity of the gospel is a cornerstone of ministry, the root of all authentic faith expression. Where there is no growth in the faith, there is no faith.

This model can be a real blessing to your church. It will demand the cooperation of many in the church, and perhaps of many churches in your area. Yet, the crisis in the Christian faith begs us to go back to the roots of our ministry to find new ways to teach the grace of God in Jesus Christ.

Chapter 11

SIGHTS AND SOUNDS: A MODEL FOR CHRISTMAS OUTREACH

The children crowded into the Snow Room. The twenty young people gazed in amazement as the giant snow person talked with them.

Suddenly one little girl spoke to the huge creature. "Hello."

"Hello," replied a deep voice. Hesitantly, the child continued the dialogue. As the group was leaving the room, the teacher pulled the director of the program to one side.

"That was a miracle!" The woman's eyes were filled with tears. "That little girl hasn't talked for several years. She has been suffering from an emotional disorder."

This dramatic experience, which took place at the Hiland Presbyterian Church, is just the tip of an amazing ministry iceberg. Jim Bell was the first minister to share this striking program with me. He developed it in York, Pennsylvania, some years ago when a teacher at a school for the disabled and emotionally disturbed in the community challenged him to find a way her students could experience the Christmas story. Jim knew that the basic senses would communicate to these students, and he designed the Sights and Sounds of Christmas at the church.

In the process of serving the children at the special school, he discovered something else quite important: Everyone loves to experience the visible Christmas story. The event was offered to the general community, and the response was fantastic! They had to hire a policeman to direct traffic. Thousands visited the week-long event!

Jim's model has been used all over the country with great

success. It is the ultimate form of the visible church as a celebration of the fact that God became visible in the Christ Child.

GOALS

1. To give visible expression to the message of Christ's birth.
2. To focus on the hospitality of the church.
3. To touch the lives of more people than at any time in the history of the church.
4. To raise the awareness that Christ is working through your church in the community.
5. To develop a foundation of experience through which the stranger can be identified and reached.
6. To focus the community within the church around a mutual ministry.

THE PLAN

This event transforms the local church into an experiential expression of God's love to the whole community. It is a labor-intensive, demanding plan. Utilizing live animals, extensive construction, and many people, the church offers something of great interest to the whole community. In this model a number of theme rooms are created in the church basement or social room.

The publicity for this event just naturally explodes. All media love this kind of visual event, and at Christmastime, they are seeking fresh stories.

ORGANIZATION

There is no way to bypass the amount of labor required by this model. Organize a planning committee a year before the Christmas season. Have the members brainstorm their version of the event. You might research what others have done, but it is important that this model be personalized to fit your situation. Someone might want to draw up plans to show how the spaces will be altered.

You will want to develop a number of teams to work on the

different aspects of the program. A great many people need to be recruited to help in getting this major celebration completed. Most people will have a limited amount of work to do, while there must be others with specialized skills—carpenters, painters, carpet layers, actors, and so on. It is helpful to remember that the process of creating an expression of the visible church is as important as the results.

The setting is simply a church basement or social room that has been transformed into a series of theme rooms. The subject matter in the rooms can take many different directions.

The most obvious experiential theme area will be the Nativity scene itself. Since the days of St. Francis the crêche (manger, animals, and holy family) has been the visible focus for the miracle of Christ's birth. One church set up its scene, with live animals and people, in the parking lot. This permitted people to look as they drove past.

At Jim's church, a large area of the basement was devoted to the nativity scene. They were able to fashion a barn-like decor and obtain live animals from a farmer. A man, a woman, and a baby appeared as the holy family. Mary and Joseph told the story of the Christ child to the group gathered in the "stable," and children could touch the donkey, the goat, and the other animals while the dialogue took place. The flow of people was regulated so that only twenty or so people were in each room at one time.

The Snow Room featured a huge white figure—a person in a white costume with a microphone. This made it possible for the snowman to talk with the visitors. Children particularly enjoyed this opportunity.

The Prayer Room had a huge tree at the center, where a box contained many blank paper "leaves." A person told a story about the power of prayer, and people filled out prayer requests and put them on the tree. Crayons were provided so that children could draw their prayer requests if they could not write.

There was a hospitality space which featured free corn bread and fresh apple cider, squeezed at the site. Hospitality of the table is a significant symbol of care.

A wide variety of rooms or spaces can be designed for this festival. The event could be built around biblical themes or historical characters. Your people will have many imaginative ideas. This "theme" park transformation of your church will thrill the people in the community.

This event is the church's gift to the community. When the thousands of people pour through your doors—and they will come in these numbers—be sure that the spirit of the Christ child can be felt by all. Each group of twenty or thirty people should have a host to guide them through this world of wonders.

How do we make strangers feel at home? What are the small things that indicate a visitor is welcome? How are children incorporated into a group? This will be the first time many people have been in your church. The impact of your Christian love will be felt by all and will determine their attitude toward the church.

Recall your feelings when you attended Disney World or Disneyland. You were carefully shepherded, at every opportunity, by numerous young people. They wanted you to have a good time.

MEDIA

You can imagine the news appeal of this event. The media folks will love it! The live nativity scene in the church will provide good pictures as well as human interest. How does it feel to play the role of Mary or Joseph? What kinds of requests do people make in the Prayer Room? How do the children respond to this sensual experience of Christmas? A special tour for children with handicaps makes a perfect story.

You might want to organize a preview for the media people. Take them through the experience just as if they were with a tour group. Find several of your articulate members who have had a great deal to do with the event. Their enthusiasm and friendliness will be perfect material for television and for the press.

It is helpful to symbolize an event like this graphically. Have an artist design a logo and use the symbol on all publicity and display advertising—bumper stickers, lapel buttons (for those who have attended), billboards, and newspaper ads. The number of impressions about the church is important. The more people hear about your loving care, the more open they will be to your message.

Some churches have found that so many people want to experience this event that free tickets needed to be issued. This is an interesting dynamic. It means that people must ask to come. The tickets are excellent visible expressions of what is happening.

The visual impression of traffic backed up around the church is another important factor. It gives the (true) impression that your church is on the move. Off-duty police will need to be hired for traffic management.

Keep a visitors' book. These names and addresses can be used for a follow-up mailing. Imagine the impact a personal invitation to the Christmas week services would have if it were mailed to each visitor during the week following the Sights and Sounds event! The list of visitors can be kept and they can be sent tickets or given the opportunity to order them for the next year's event.

AFTERWARD

The successful completion of an event like this deserves a special celebration by and for those who have put it together. This can best be done by the congregation at worship on the following Sunday. Stories from the volunteers concerning things that happened during the event can be shared. How has God worked through this experience? What blessings have come to us through these strangers?

Encourage people in the congregation to stand and express their feelings. What happened to them as a result of hosting this gathering? What does the stranger need from the message of Christ?

AND SO . . .

This model is within reach of every church. It takes a great amount of labor but little money. The sensual experience of Christ's birthday is a special event for everyone in the community. Both young and old will flock to see it. The process of making the faith visible to others is at the very heart of the visible church.

The living Christmas event also underscores that the truly visible church is the work of many people. No leader can do this kind of community effort alone. The dream must belong to the whole church. This kind of teamwork means that a group of people can create more than one person alone. It also means that many people will have a deep investment in the ministry. It will be their work.

Chapter 12

MODELS FOR
LENT, PALM SUNDAY,
GOOD FRIDAY

The church year is one of the most stimulating and exciting gifts of God. The fact that we can be nudged along in our faith understanding, through signposts that mark the mighty works of God, is a blessing for those concerned with the visible church. These steps for celebrating God's love are reasons to break from the ordinary way of doing things. Even those churches that never have become visible in an intentional way will be ready for something special.

Three models guide us in the process of using the Easter season in a special way to touch the lives of others.

LENT

The weeks from Ash Wednesday to Easter have been a traditional time of preparation for Christians. Many Protestants have rejected the elaborate acts of spiritual exercise which had been developed through the years. Yet, more and more contemporary Christians would like to get back to the roots of spiritual renewal. They long to embrace something of meaning. How can the trappings of material security be released so that they can embrace the love of Jesus Christ?

I was approached by a group of churches concerning this aspect of Lent. They knew that families find it difficult to develop a routine of prayer and Bible study. Everyone is busy, and often there is a bit of embarrassment among too many Christians concerning conversation about faith. But they knew also that the Lenten season offers a natural bridge between our daily needs and the rich legacy of spiritual power that is ours in Jesus Christ.

Goals

I developed a Lenten series of devotional materials designed to meet the needs of those people. There are three goals for this program:

1. To provide daily devotional material which involves both young and old.
2. To provide an opportunity to offer prayer and biblical devotional material to others in the community.
3. To provide an opportunity for church people to reach out to others.

How does one begin to move people into a pattern that will result in this kind of devotional life? When can an intergenerational gathering be found in most homes? How can both young and old be included in a process of a faith experience?

Since we were trying to reach both young and old in family settings, the time that seemed to best fit our needs was mealtime. Most family units have one meal together each day. It may be breakfast or dinner, and we do not assume that the units were biologically related. It was important only that they be at the same table.

The question of content was answered by our conviction that the Bible was our focus. However, how could both small children and experienced adults be included in a participatory manner?

A few years ago I stumbled across an approach to Bible study which provided an excellent answer. The safest way to study the Bible is to let the actual text suggest how it should be studied! In other words, use materials which literally draw their teaching method from the passage being studied.*

This intentional approach to Bible study and devotional material is very exciting. The Bible is very experiential. It pulses with emotion, sensual awareness, and spiritual power. The texts are just waiting to be released in ways through which the believer can experience the love of God.

A kit with daily devotional exercises was produced. But I knew that the family table should be prepared in such a way that this new activity would be appreciated and anticipated, and we came

---

*Dennis Benson, *Creative Bible Studies* (Loveland, Colo.: Group Books, 1985)

up with a piece which could be turned into a visible symbol of the Lenten journey.

Ann Williamson, an artist friend, designed a sheet with beautifully styled fishes, which could focus the devotional time. In the instructions, we asked each family unit to wrap a milk carton or plastic container with a piece of newspaper and tape it at the edges. Over this slice of life from the world, the fishes designed by Ann could be placed on the sides of the emerging centerpiece.

It also became apparent that the walk to Easter needed to be marked by service. We were following Christ, who calls us to be servants. We suggested that a slot could be cut in the side or top of the transformed milk carton. Coins could be collected in the centerpiece at each devotional gathering, and the collection could be presented on Easter Sunday to feed the hungry.

Here are seven of those devotional exercises. They will give a sense of what this kit contained. You could use this model, but have your members create their own exercises. At a pre-Lenten family night, have the people present form new family units. Hand out the devotionals and ask each unit to do one. Then give each family unit a passage and let each create an exercise. These can be collected, edited, and distributed in your own kit to all the families in the church.

1. *Psalm 102:9-10*. Read the text. Give each person a paper match. Ask the diners to split the layers of paper to form a stick figure (arms and legs with match top being the head). This shape represents a moment of sadness or bitterness experienced by the diners today or in the past week. Share the stories. Place all the match figures in an ash tray and set them afire as you lead a circle prayer asking God to burn away the sin which taints your lives.

2. *Matthew 17:24-27*. Read the text. Pass the centerpiece around the table and invite the diners to share the first thoughts that come into their heads as the fish in the decoration are studied. Then pass around a coin and ask the diners to share the ways the coin symbolizes God's special care for them during this day. Pray for those who may not have money to pay taxes or electricity at this time of the year. Invite a person who has never been a guest at dinner to eat with you at the next meal.

3. *Genesis 18:1-8*. You will need a washcloth and bowl of warm water. Read the text. Ask each person to wash the hands of the next person. Set the bread before the guest you have invited to the dinner and ask that person to share words of hope and good news for those at the table. End with circle prayer.

4. *Matthew 25:31-37*. Read the text. Pass the centerpiece around the table. Ask each person to look at the newspaper in which the milk carton has been wrapped and share some part of the world's need which the words of Jesus could address in our day. Conclude with circle prayer concerning the hungry, thirsty, lonely, naked, sick, and imprisoned of our world.

5. *Matthew 6:9-13*. Ask each person to offer one verse of the text (the Lord's Prayer) as you go around the table. Pass a loaf of bread and ask each person to break off a piece. Tell them this is the debtor's bread. Ask the diners to share one debt or sin which they have committed against another. Eat the pieces together and conclude by saying that God has provided this bread and that it symbolizes our forgiveness of sin. Suggest that the diners undertake a brief fast—no snacks or other food from early lunch until the next meal at which you gather.

6. *Proverbs 4:17-19*. Read the text. Pass around a loaf of bread and a cup which contains grape juice or wine. Ask each person to smell the contents of the cup and look at its color. Tell them this is the wine of violence. Ask them to share a story it suggests from their own lives concerning wickedness. Focus on our omission of service of love toward neighbor, family member, or stranger. Ask each person to break off a piece of bread, dip the piece into the cup, and eat.

7. *Hosea 4:1-3*. Read the text. Place a large bowl of water on the table. Pour ink and other coloring agents into it. Ask each person to look at the water and share examples of how we have destroyed the environment through the misuse of our resources. Discuss how such a situation represents the sin we have committed against God. Close with prayer circle for the gift of nature. Give each person a shiny apple. Suggest that it be given to a stranger with a blessing.

Forty of these devotional exercises were placed in each kit, which were purchased by the churches in the area. The kits were also utilized as an evangelism tool by many churches. Each worshiper was given three kits during the Sunday service before the beginning of Lent. A sheet listing the Lenten services of the local church had been added to each envelope, and members were urged to give the kits to people in their neighborhood, with an invitation to join them for worship.

And So . . .

This simple model can be of great use. It helps the congregation develop its own spiritual depth and provides a gentle way to reach out to others. This model does not employ electronic media, but it does provide a solid foundation for outreach. The people of God must be prepared to offer the gospel for others.

The visible church can communicate only that which it truly possesses. It must continually strengthen itself spiritually in order to provide the experience of the gospel for others.

THE KING IS COMING:
A PALM SUNDAY PARADE

This model for the visible church was developed by Douglas Alder, one of my students, for the churches in his community. Let's follow it and see where it will lead us.

Doug felt that the churches in the local community were missing the excitement and power of Christ's triumphant entry into Jerusalem on the way to the cross, a biblical event that is a mixture of joyous acknowledgment of Christ's kingship and the sad prelude to his suffering and death. Those who celebrated with him soon turned against him. This experience is the gateway to the Easter garden miracle. Doug wanted to provide an experience that would bring the impact of that event to his town.

Goals

1. To stimulate interest in the message of Palm Sunday among the churches of the community.
2. To stimulate interest in the Holy Week message among the unchurched.

Doug envisioned this model as including several churches from different traditions. The event would start at 9:30 A.M., the usual starting time for early worship at one of the churches. The members of that church and people from the other churches would meet there for "The Gathering."

The congregation would leave the sanctuary of that church after the "Call to Worship" and begin a "Proclamation" parade, led by a riderless white donkey. Persons on the parade route could join in. Marchers would be given palm branches and song sheets. The parade would continue to another sponsoring church, where it would stop for the reading of selections from Mark 11, Luke 19, and John 12.

The collected congregation would then move on to the next church. Perhaps a drum or some other musical instrument could be used for singing and cadence. A drum and bugle corps could be asked to provide this musical accompaniment. It is amazing how cooperative people in the community are when the church suggests something exciting and creative.

The parade would end at the third church with a conclusion to the movable worship service. The final response of the congregation will be the release of helium-filled balloons. The worshipers would sing the *Alleluia* chant before the benediction.

Every person would be given a lapel pin imprinted with a palm branch. These pins would be worn during the next week, and when asked what it meant, church members would have an opportunity to share their faith in the risen Lord and invite others to church for the Holy Week activities. This will give the people in the church a chance to witness to the miracle of Easter Sunday. Many people in the contemporary church are not accustomed to discussing their faith, and this pin would make it easy for them to reach out in this way.

Media

Doug envisions an extensive media outreach in his community. The newspaper is a key media opportunity. A series of "teaser" advertisements would run daily, or several in one issue, suggesting that someone special was coming: "Watch for Him!" "Listen for Him!" It is important that the ad campaign really create curiosity. A final large ad would announce the special parade and feature a picture of the donkey.

Radio would also be an important part of the campaign. Again, local stations are very cooperative. They will give special rates, help in production,and give a good analysis of the audience. Be sure to bargain.

Posters, bumper stickers, and strong promotion in all the churches are important factors in this outreach model. Nothing can replace the energy such an event receives from person-to-person invitations and support. Mass-media promotion of a local church event tends to make members of the congregation proud of what their church is doing, and they then become more invitational with their friends.

Television stations will also be looking for fresh ways to report Palm Sunday. They usually get shots from inside a church. This model offers some excellent outdoor opportunities. The usual preparation and consistent work with producers will obtain some good coverage.

This model offers a few special problems. When planning an outside event, weather is always an uncertainty. You will be biting your nails until the last minute. Some special preparations also must undergird your plan. The local police force will be a necessary partner in your scheme. Some communities demand a parade permit, but there are usually clear procedures for getting such permission.

If there isn't an existing cooperative spirit among the churches in the community, you would have to trigger this in some way. On the other hand, I have found that the best way to pull a group of people together is to focus on a common project. This model might be the very thing your community has been needing in order to make the Christian faith visible.

This model offers an excellent opportunity to make visible an event that has so much drama and power. The joyous reception of Jesus foreshadows his humiliation and triumphant moment, the resurrection. This roller coaster of human experience is something to which everyone can relate. In fact, these difficult times of sudden change in social, political, and economic status demand a faith that is solid. The message of the Easter event will be welcomed by those who are lost and confused.

STATIONS OF THE CROSS MARCH:
A GOOD FRIDAY MODEL

The roll of drums echoed through the hills, the cadence slow and deliberate. People came streaming out of stores, cars, and homes. From the perspective of a helicopter, a solemn procession could be discerned in the swelling crowds along the street. A man in the center of the teeming crowd could be seen dragging a huge cross.

This piece of news tape, the lead story on the 11:00 evening news, perfectly captured the moving power of this ecumenical Good Friday pilgrimage. In fact, the film story was featured on all the locals stations, and also appeared on the morning and early evening news the next day. The newspapers also gave the event extensive coverage.

That Good Friday march was designed by a coalition of Protestant and Catholic churches in a major city. Their neighborhood wasn't the best. The mills were down, and the houses were old. The people were poor, but the rest of the city didn't seem to notice the spiritual vitality and hope they possessed.

The pastors and church leaders of the community had worked together in the past on projects of mutual concern. How could they send a message to the broken and confused world concerning the role of Jesus Christ in their lives? What was the common starting point they all shared in their faith? How could God use them to reach the whole city?

The leaders from the different churches worked together to develop this public worship celebration. They found that a united witness to the death and resurrection of Jesus Christ was an important statement to make to the world.

Goals

The Stations of the Cross March had several goals:

1. To proclaim the saving power of God through the death and resurrection of Jesus Christ.
2. To bring the impact of this message to the people in their neighborhood community.

3. To demonstrate the united witness of the Christian community.
4. To make an impact on the larger metropolitan community through media coverage.

Organization

These leaders developed the march route, which began at one church and ended at another several miles away. Along the way they created seven "signs" or "stations." At each point the marchers stopped, Scripture was read, and a symbolic act was performed upon the person bearing the cross.

A different pastor oversaw each of these devotional spots. There was also a change in the person bearing the cross, to show that we all bear the cross of Christ. At one stop, nails were driven into the crossbeam. The heavy hammer made an incredible sound as the nails were driven home, and a visible shudder rippled across the large crowd. The people along the route were extremely attentive. Even the young men standing on the street corners were caught up in the sweep of this dramatic pageant. The power of this part of the church year was felt by everyone present.

The drums accompanied a slow change as the march moved along the route. It was amazing how many people followed the procession into the church for a short service, where people were given an opportunity to share their reflections on Good Friday.

A reception was held after the service in the basement of the host church. This gave the people from the churches and from the community a chance for fellowship to celebrate their oneness in this experience.

Media

Representatives from the organizing committee contacted media producers and editors well before the event. They then visited each of these people with maps and an outline of the plan. This was important for the television stations, which needed to plan helicopter coverage.

The media were assigned individual hosts who helped them negotiate the route and obtain interviews from different spokespeople. This helped them obtain the material they needed and also gave representatives from each church a chance to be interviewed on behalf of this ecumenical event.

AND SO . . .

This is an excellent example of ways the natural rhythm of the events of the Christian year can be turned inside out to touch others. There is such authentic drama in the acts of salvation! Just making the stories of God's action in our lives visible makes an impact on society.

The Good Friday model also points out the power of undertaking ministry as a united witness. The general ecumenical movement seems to have stalled in its traditional format. Local councils of churches and related national and international groups have fallen on hard times.

Yet the spirit of Christian cooperation is still strong. I have found that brothers and sisters in Christ now gather together in common mission more comfortably than ever before. The big difference is that today the ecumenical spirit is focused on ministry the parties know they can't do alone. This means that grassroots cooperative ministry thrives. The dangers of this pragmatic approach is that the larger national and international dimensions of ministry cannot be addressed.

It is still a discerning experience to realize that Christ has created a new kind of kinship. You may be personally closer in theological outlook to someone from another tradition than to a person in your own church with the same theological training and tradition. The reality of this unity in Christ makes a powerful statement to those outside the faith.

This plan also takes media involvement seriously in its intentional visibility. The elements of newsworthiness emerge naturally from the content. The organizers have bonded form and content almost organically in this model.

The Stations of the Cross March will enrich the Easter season for you and for others.

Chapter 13

A HOT SUMMER: THREE MODELS

"What do you want to do?"

"I don't know. What do you want to do?"

This snatch of dialogue could have been taken from a 1950s movie or could be what all young persons still say on a summer night in most American towns and cities. Even in a time of hi-tech and television, most young people are bored, or out of work and bored. The churches' programming concept is built around some unfortunate assumptions when it comes to summertime. They accept as reality that summer is simply a vacation time for religion. This dip in intentional church programming may stem from the rural cycle of farming or from the upper-class pattern of the past when people would go away for the whole summer.

It is true that tense work schedules, seven-day work patterns, and weekend escapes have made the historical assumption true once again for some. However, it has generally been the churches' willingness to go into hibernation during the summer that has led to the paralyzed church during that season.

The traffic is terrible. People are fighting to get into the shopping center. Yet there is more to this tie-up than just a bad evening at the mall. Saint Thomas More Catholic Church is changing the traffic patterns and visibly making a statement about the gospel. It is packing the church with worshipers on Saturday night!

Catholic parishes across the country have given us an inspiring example of a way the visible church can respond to the changing needs of the community. They have been offering worship services at times when the people can most readily attend.

Theological subtleties can lead to differences in worship practices. However, the world has shifted in its work, leisure, and spiritual patterns. History helps us. If we look back at our theological forebears, we find that they worship in every possible setting and circumstance. Our praise of God can never be limited by cultural prejudices and habits.

Many Protestant churches are offering visible signs of worship for the times. Family services, early morning worship, and other liturgical responses to people's needs are appearing across the country. Many churches have celebrated in parks and camp grounds, to provide summer worship for visitors. There is exciting ministry going on in many places.

I. THE PICNIC:
A MODEL FOR SUMMER

The church picnic is one of the oldest and most revered programming models of the church. Perhaps Jesus hosted the first picnic when he preached to the five thousand. The ice-cream social, the corn feast, the pancake supper, and many other annual events are stables in many local communities.

Let's view the typical church picnic from the perspective of the visible church in the media age. Several goals seem obtainable and worthwhile:

1. To create a climate of hospitality in which the love of Christ may be experienced by member and stranger, young and old.
2. To provide a climate of celebration and fun in which the fellowship of Christ may be experienced by member and stranger, young and old.
3. To draw more people to The Picnic than to any other event in the church's history.

The key to accomplishing these goals is participation. The more people who help to prepare and promote the event, the better it will work. Prayer and spiritual preparation are vital. This can be undertaken through existing prayer groups, the housebound, Sunday morning worship, and more. How do we prepare the way of the Lord's hospitality? It is vital that the church not see The Picnic merely as a time for itself. The guests at the event are extremely important. The stranger is coming to our home. How do we treat those whom God has sent?

Organization

A well-planned gathering such as this is very labor intensive. Yet people will accept responsibility for a single, highly defined task. You can also ask for participation according to skills, interests, and enjoyment. When the event becomes The Picnic for them, members will be more likely to invite their friends and neighbors outside the church.

Don't forget how successfully the well-run theme parks have created the illusion of hospitality. In Disney World there seems to be someone always at your elbow to assist you. You are pampered and cared for at every point.

The church bases such intentional attitudes of hospitality on the concept of servanthood. We are called by Christ to be servant to stranger and neighbor. Of course, the guest always blesses the host or hostess in the process of such giving.

Food. A good picnic needs food—good food. Many churches have an unbelievable reservoir of great recipes and great cooks. It is easiest to be thematic (roast pig, barbecued ribs, catfish, etc.) for marketing purposes. However, other folks have found great success in featuring the best recipes of their members, when everyone brings a favorite dish.

Spiritual Climate. Yet we do not celebrate the hospitality of Christ with bread alone. It is "in the breaking of the bread" that we feast on the fellowship of the table. You may want to provide hosts at each table so that strangers are included in the table talk. It is very tempting for a church to have a picnic in which friends sit together and others are left to fend for themselves. But The Picnic is an outreach, an inclusive experience. Members may need to be trained so they can undertake their important role comfortably.

Play. You also will need a focused center of play, which can take many forms—contests, music, sports, and so on. If you decide on games, I strongly suggest that you deemphasize competition. Utilize activities that are inclusive of age groups and levels of physical ability. Many exciting models for these kinds of games can be found in books and other resources. Will your activities guarantee that participants won't be embarrassed, excluded, endangered, or become losers?

Setting. It is tempting to bring up the tables from the basement. Yet, many churches have been able to transform simple outdoor space into a space of wonder. For instance, one church tied The Picnic to a reunion. Everyone who had been a member over the years was contacted and invited to come back for this summer expression of the visible church. In fact, the invitation was made general and nonmembers who had moved away were also asked to come.

These visitors were encouraged to bring a picture of themselves at the time they first attended the church or lived in the community. The pictures were posted and everyone was given a sheet with boxes and a place to write in the name when they had guessed the person in each picture.

Tents, parachutes, and plastic structures can make amazing transformations. Lighting, banners, and other modifications can create a revival tent of yesteryear or a spaceship of the future. Notice the floats that young people have constructed of chicken wire and tissue paper for parades.

Pleasant music can create a positive aural environment for the event. It is best to have live music, but it is often difficult for performers to provide background to activities focused on something else. One church group actually used an environmental record that provided heightened sounds of nature.

Worship. Worship is always appropriate when the people of God meet. However, it may have different expressions in different settings. This model is not designed to be a revival or a secular theme park. The worship moments must fit into the setting. A blessing format could be designed to be led by the hosts at each table, or a closing blessing would be suitable. If The Picnic is outside and informal, informal worship is most appropriate.

Media

The event needs to be symbolized in a logo which captures its spirit and is easy to recognize. This graphic can be displayed on banners, posters, lapel pins, and billboards. A local artist can work with you on this. It is helpful to remember that the logo must be seen at a distance. Is it recognizable from afar and when reduced for print? Is it simple, so that its message is easily communicated? Will it look good in one color?

It is vital that you use the same logo or form of the print to announce The Picnic every time it appears. This consistency helps the public identify your event. The importance of this concept can be seen in the intense battles that have been waged over trademarks. A product's name and the art style of the letters will be defended at great cost.

The Picnic has a fun, informal feel, so you might want to use a promotional approach in keeping with its nature. For instance, you might create a fun handbill to be put in doors of houses and under windshields, as well as in the church bulletin. Do check local restrictions since towns have ordinances against such distribution.

If you follow the theme for The Picnic, you will find a great angle for newspapers. Imagine the intriguing stories that could be gathered from those out-of-towners! If you can get the phone numbers of some key visitors, you could encourage the newspapers to do interviews *before* The Picnic. The people who will attend your event offer the best media stories, and you will need to help the media people discover these angles.

The polish and glitter of stories on national media tend to make us feel that our tales are not very interesting, but the faith community has the most important material in existence! The older widow who works with Meals on Wheels is friendly and loving to all. She fights a shrinking income, crippling arthritis, and loneliness with hope and faith. She is a heroine, and only you can find these kind people for the mass-media folks.

And So . . .

This model is one of the oldest and most obvious ways to be the visible church in the summer. Yet it can also be a fresh and wonderful way to touch the lives of others. It will take the sensibilities of the visible church to give it special impact on the people of our world.

The electronic media and newspapers may do their major

coverage *after* the event. This is still an excellent exposure for the message of the visible church. Seeds of awareness will be sown for your next presentation of The Picnic.

There is another aftermath strategy for The Picnic. You might want to give people a chance to communicate that they attended this special event. Notice how the T-shirt has expressed this for musical concerts. This is a way of visibly communicating that you were there when the concert took place. This same dynamic can be related to The Picnic. The T-shirts that represent your event can be designed and sold. People will love this symbol of a special time.

II. A VERY HOT SUMMER:
ANOTHER MODEL

Floyd Shaffer, the father of theological clowning, is a dear friend who has given the church a wonderful legacy. He has demonstrated that the symbol of the clown can be utilized to communicate and discover the gospel for our time. The Bible and the liturgy of the church have been his benchmark. How can one combine training of the senses with playfulness in order to present Christ to others? No one has provided more answers to this question than Floyd.

Several years ago he and a group of friends went into a part of the country that was embroiled in a labor dispute. Migrant workers, a farm union, and farmers were struggling in a sometimes three-way battle. It was a tense, hot summer.

Floyd and his folks are convinced that the image of the clown is christological. They had demonstrated that the clown can be an agent of healing and love, and in this farm setting they faced the new challenge of being ambassadors of reconciliation.

They had been invited into the community by several of the churches. It was clear that they had to begin with the children. The team utilized the basic tools of clowning: mime, play, music, and dance.

Quickly the summer of discontent took on a new edge for the young people. They were bored during their free time, and they welcomed these loving and sharing people. The clowns enabled the young people to find new ways to communicate. Creative skills were uncovered and nurtured in the farm children. Parents began to be drawn into the activities—mime, play, creative exercises, and the like.

When the growing group of young people and adults studied the roots of reconciliation, they decided to sponsor a festival of love. The event that resulted touched the whole community. All the parties to the labor dispute even participated together.

The event opened with a parade of young people in clown makeup. Their costumes were created from used items and common clothing worn in a humorous way. The clowns played a couple of numbers on their bazoos, then passed out the toy instruments to the crowd of adults. It was a delightful time of sharing and community.

There was no intention to utilize this summer ministry as a media outreach. The community did not want the attention of the news agencies of the world. The people needed a chance to work on their difficulties in their own way. Yet, this is the kind of story a producer would beg for. This model excludes the usual mass-media component deliberately.

And So . . .

This model may seem so peculiar that you would not or could not duplicate it. Yet it demonstrates that the outlook of the visible church can offer a ministry perspective to touch the vital center of Christ's presence in every encounter of life. What are the pinch points in your community? How can the gospel reach out to embrace these hurts and visibly demonstrate the love of Christ?

III. Super Summer:
A Third Model

A congregation in Maryland fights the usual summer church blahs by intentional outreach. The members conduct The Super Summer youth ministry program. Instead of closing down the youth group, they hire college students and offer a full *daily* program. For instance, there is a five-day junior high program each week. The youths go canoeing, see museums, and share other adventures.

Even young adults are included; they meet at a time that

permits them to work. From this mix of excitement has come the Tent Troupe. This band of adults and young people perform plays drawn from the professional list (*The Diary of Anne Frank*, etc.) across a several state area. They purchased a theater tent, generators, and other equipment, so when hosted by local churches in the areas they visit, the Tent Troupe requires only a vacant lot and strong promotion from the local sponsor. A children's play is given in the afternoon, an adult play in the evening, and time is allotted for the audience to converse with the cast. This has been an incredible summer outreach program.

Media

This program is highly promoted. The weekly mailings to community youth are lively, sparkling, and compelling. The church even publishes a summer directory of phone numbers so the young people can call each other.

There is an abundance of young people, and even with vacations and work, most of them have time on their hands. Strong programming and belief that such a program is needed tend to generate a positive reaction.

The experience of this church has proved that direct mail is the key medium for reaching the participants in this program. Young people love to receive personalized mail. With desk-top publishing, a whole new world of possibility for print promotion and outreach has opened. The visible church must be expressed impeccably through print. With the computer, there is no excuse.

And So . . .

This model is needed in just about every community. Any community could carry it out ecumenically. But there is subtlety to this outreach—it involves more than the "keeping the kids off the street" attitude that has fueled most youth ministry. The program must be challenging, meaningful, and exciting.

Summer cannot be wasted in this time of extreme human suffering. Work camps, service projects, and volunteer service are opportunities the visible church needs to explore continuously.

Chapter 14

THE CIRCLE OF HOPE: AN ADVENT MODEL

The snow-swept countryside slowly unfolds as a lone horse and rider move across the screen. "It is 1776. The times and the people are hard." With these images and words, the heart of an intense outreach program was broadcast throughout western Pennsylvania, eastern Ohio, and northern West Virginia. Four months of intense work and risk had brought the program to this point.

A group of Presbyterians had founded a media agency to serve a three-state area and, through a series of unexpected occurrences, had received a grant of $66,000 to begin work. How does one start a new media ministry? How can the church be awakened to the possibilities of using mass media as a part of the ministry of the local congregation? How does a mainline denomination differ from a free-lance evangelist on television in its message and style of work?

The board of directors struggled with these questions. I suggested that we create a visible outreach plan. The target audience would be the 450,000 Presbyterians and the people outside the church in the three-state area. The Circle of Hope was the result. This multifaceted campaign would cost $35,000. There was an intense discussion. "We didn't earn this money, nor seek it very aggressively. It seems as if God has given it to us. I move that we go for it." The pastor of a large church expressed the thoughts of everyone.

The people in our area were facing the first significant impact of what would become the Rust Belt. The big mills were beginning to close. A decade of pain and terror for our region was well on its way. Families would be separated, homes would be lost, marriages would collapse, and dreams of college would be abandoned in the wake of this third wave of change. All illusions of hope would be lost forever in the minds of our people.

It seemed to us that the best way to begin to reach out in the contemporary world was to relate the courage of the past to the present. The Presbyterians in our area had a long and distinguished history. As I researched the documents of the period, I was amazed that so many of our contemporary issues were similar to those of these early Christians, yet they faced enormous odds and personal tragedy with courage and faith.

I learned also that those hardy forebears were much more holistic in their outlook than the folks who wore the denominational label today. They rode into the area of western Pennsylvania in 1776 and immediately established schools where people could learn Greek and Latin, the basic foundations of an educated society.

The pioneer pastors became deeply involved in politics because there were no governmental authorities. In fact, one of the pastors was drawn into the Whiskey Rebellion when he urged the men not to bear arms against the government forces attempting to impose national whiskey tax. (He later conducted their funerals.)

In another important response to hard times, those feisty frontier Christians left accounts of four-hour revivals, in which the Spirit of God was so active that the people would not leave. Those ancestors in the faith must have been intellectuals, social activists, and also spiritual giants. Our contemporaries usually choose one of those three gifts as the focus of their Christian life.

GOALS

I also wanted to use a variety of means to reach the consciousness of the target audience. There were three goals for The Circle of Hope:

1. To communicate a sense of historical Christian hope to contemporary people who are often hopeless in the face of problems.

2. To raise awareness in the people who received this message
   that this means of communication could serve the ministry
   of the local church.
3. To raise awareness in the community that the Presbyterian
   Church is faithful to the message of Jesus Christ.

The plan for the visible outreach of this faith community was
the circle of relationships into which Christ draws every person.
This kinship is based on what God did and is doing through Jesus
Christ. The continuity of this extended family is based on the
past, present, and future, but the people drawn into its company
are joined by spiritual kinship, not genetic linkage. It is the blood
of Jesus Christ that bonds us into this spiritual family circle of
hope and love. We decided to make visible this special kinship
by beginning with our particularity and history. We would then
move to the inclusive community, which transcends racial,
ethnic, social, and denominational specifics.

It was decided that the faith history would provide the best
foundation for a view of hope touching the present and future.
We did not want to offer a public picture of the Scotch-Irish
settlers and their spiritual children of today. Biblical hope is
more than optimism or possibility thinking. We knew that
Christian hope is inseparably blended into the reality of
suffering, pain, and courage. Hope is the reality that God works
in history. This is not nostalgia, the emotional remembrance of
how we wished things had been. Christian hope is the story of
God's people and what God is doing and has done through them.
It is through this kind of hope that we experience anew that God
is faithful and gracious.

THE MOVIE

This plan focused on the production of a major television film.
A thirty-minute script was written around an event which took
place in November 1776. Our "Little House on the Prairie"
format utilized authentic costumes, the actual house in which the
event took place, and professional actors. We were lucky that the
historical society had preserved the homestead and all the
furnishings, and even had gathered clothing from the period.
The difficult conditions of the times are revealed by the

characters. The fear of war, hunger, moral decay, and illness surrounds these isolated people.

We spent hours interviewing actors. It seemed that every actor in the area wanted a role. Stage actors don't have many opportunities to act before the camera. The technique is different, and the director of the film company we chose aided us on this matter. "If they don't have pictures with them, we won't have a chance of remembering the individual candidates." He was right. After nine hours of interviewing, I couldn't remember which person had read what.

We finally cast the film and chose location spots at the Miller Homestead, the Chartiers cemetery, a horse shed, and a farm in Washington County. We had only two days to shoot the script.

I learned how hard it is to produce such a project. We had a cast and crew of fifty people to feed and transport, along with two horses, a small baby, and numerous other items to be arranged along the way.

During the filming, the Beatles were suddenly singing in the middle of a tender 1776 scene. We had to negotiate with the neighborhood roller rink to turn down their music system.

The actor playing the lead role of the frontier minister suddenly announced that he would be leaving in sixty minutes. He knew we had his big scene to shoot, but he had to make the curtain for that evening's presentation of *Dracula*.

There was one item for $3.75 on the expense log, labeled "horse makeup." We used two horses because the one in the stable scene couldn't be ridden. One horse had a white blaze on its face which had to be made up to match the brown face of the other horse! The film was edited and prepared for airing.

William Rusch, executive of the Synod of the Trinity, spoke in a sixty-second epilogue to connect the courage of the past to the trials facing society today. Slides of seven different ministries in response to these problems were shown as he spoke.

Media

We began our rounds of local television stations in the quest for air time and found that the network affiliates were not available at the time we sought, 8:00 P.M., the first Sunday of Advent. They would not break into prime time for a thirty-minute film, and the cost of time was outrageous. The electric evangelists had literally bid against one another for available time and forced the rates up.

So we bargained with the powerful independent VHF station, which served a 75-mile area around our market. The station signed a contract for the 8:00 P.M. slot, but warned us that it would be preempted if someone purchased a full hour that coincided with our slot. This meant that we had to undertake our multifaceted plan without being sure the main piece would air on that date.

To symbolize the Circle of Hope, we created a logo formed by a human hand's thumb and forefinger, touching. The other three digits were extended straight up. "All of creation is within God's circle of hope. The other three fingers stand for the trinity."

This logo was used on our lapel buttons, print pieces, video images, and other materials. The design on the button showed only the fingers. This striking design acted as a "teaser," or unknown element. What did it mean? Curious people asked about it, and the folks wearing the buttons then had a chance to talk about their faith and invite the inquirer to church on Advent Sunday. At least 109,000 buttons were distributed to Presbyterians across the three-state area.

Three years later I bumped into an older gentleman from a small church. He didn't know me, and when I asked him about the Circle of Hope button he was wearing, he launched into his personal witness to Jesus Christ! When I told him about my involvement in creating the campaign, he related how he had used the button to talk with people about the faith. He felt it had enabled him to take the blessing of Christ to many people.

As many as 125,000 bulletin inserts with a special litany of dedication were sent to churches in the area to encourage folks to invite others to watch the TV show and come to the Advent activities of the church. On the other side of the insert was a study guide for those watching the show, and it was suggested that they create viewing groups. Visitors and neighbors were invited to the 150 groups established by churches for this purpose.

Bill Aber, a church executive, wrote a special Advent devotional guide that included stories of hope with biblical reflections on the time. This handsome guide was offered in the churches and to the viewers during the show. Several thousands were distributed.

A few weeks before the television showing, a special premiere of the film was held in a movie theatre, with several relatives of the historical characters in the film present. Church leaders were invited from across the region, and in spite of a snowstorm on that day, seventy-five people attended the showing.

We organized a bank of telephones at the regional church offices to answer calls the night of the show. The people recruited to answer were church officials and others who needed to learn how media could be used. I wanted them to own this new ministry and to experience personally the impact of the program on the public. This was a dangerous strategy. What if people hated it?

But one hundred people called after the show! Others wrote to say that they either were proud to be Presbyterians or were non-Presbyterians pleased with the message we were presenting. Many people related to aspects of the story. Several indicated that young folks in their family had gone astray: "I wish my grandson would listen to me the way the young fellow in the story respected his grandmother."

AND SO . . .

The Circle of Hope played a major role in launching the Presbyterian Media Mission. It is now a vital media unit which produces two nationally syndicated radio shows heard weekly on 190 stations, as well as print and video materials. The Religious Public Relationships Council bestowed the Wilbur Award on The Circle of Hope as the best regionally produced media campaign.

The Circle of Hope demonstrates that one's peculiar history can be a blessing of outreach for a wider public community. There was an intentional inclusive quality to the campaign—this point is very important for the church at this time.

Unfortunately, an inner-directed attitude which has an almost "ethnocentric" quality flourishes currently among most mainline churches. They want to talk only to themselves. This attitude has been nurtured by national church officers who are trying to persuade the local congregations to support their work.

But a strong grassroots character has grown from the decentralization thrust of the culture, encouraged by leaders who have not lead. It is local energy that is the key to every successful plan. We will not be saved by a national office. Even the most supportive and most helpful person there cannot know the dynamics and resources of the local area as well as a local person does. If you don't know them, you can find out in a week of listening.

The story that God works through the lives of a given people has universal implication if shared in an inclusive way. Our only legitimate communication task as the visible church is to proclaim Jesus Christ. If our messages are lifegiving, people will know where they come from.

Pepsi, Coke, and others really serious about swaying the public to their cause communicate the (alleged) *benefits* of their products. They almost never talk about the product itself, but show swarms of healthy, attractive young people having fun, experiencing love and happiness, with their product in the center of all this mythology. They let the stories do the selling.

It is interesting that Jesus also let the experience of his message move the listeners. The power of a parable or event was shown to the listeners, who were able to respond to the impact it made on their lives.

You are in an extremely powerful position to make an extraordinary impact on your community. Your peculiar story as a faith tradition is your best content. Just let the benefits of living this faith through the story of its people be shared. Trust that the demonstration of God's love working through your kinship will touch others.

You don't need to be ashamed of your particularity or desperate about the necessity of bragging about it. The Circle of Hope was a real blessing to all involved.

Chapter 15

THE CARE CORPS:
A MODEL OF VISIBLE
YOUTH SERVICE

"I just don't know what to do. When I turn the leadership of the youth group over to the kids, they just want social events."

"Our kids are caught up in the hyperactivity of our community and only want the right clothes and things affluence can bring."

"The youths in our church are into a very narrow spiritual pattern. They are concerned about their own salvation and are not able to reach out to others."

These diverse comments reflect the kinds of situations I keep bumping into during my travels around the country. Youth ministry leaders often are perplexed over finding a holistic pattern for faith development. How can they balance the social, spiritual, and serving aspects of youth work with a given group of young people? In fact, not many adults can provide models of the complete Christian life for the younger members of the church.

The fragmentation of secular culture has infected the life of many congregations. Local church programming seems to segment people's lives so that they are offered only pieces of the Christian life. An educational experience takes place on Wednesday evening, a worship opportunity on Sunday morning, a social option on Saturday, or a service experience on Saturday.

This salad-bar approach has advantages in terms of marketing and flexibility, but the holistic bundle of energy in Acts 2:39-42 seems a more wholesome pattern. After the Pentecost sermon by Peter, the new Christians and others gathered around tables and shared in the whole Christian life—study, fellowship, worship—and then went out to serve/proclaim.

The real danger of the diffused church program, in terms of

theology, is that this diversity of interests in the separate parts of the community fails to touch the whole body. Diversity of gifts has real theological significance only in the context of the shared life. In other words, one needs to experience grace working through particular aspects of the ministry which are undertaken through the faithfulness of others. Without this communion with other parts of the body, the Christian life is incomplete.

During the past five years I have interviewed hundreds of people who have had amazing religious experiences. One woman told me about the time she was told by the doctors that she was dying: "I was praying. I put myself in God's hand and a strange sensation filled me. I felt a pressure all around me. I could hear the beating of angels' wings. I must have fallen asleep. When the doctors came, they said my heart sounded different. Well, here I am today. God healed me."

I have never had an experience like that, but I was awed to be in that woman's presence and believe her witness. I am thankful I could share a part of the Christian life I never have known personally.

A man told me how the Spirit of Christ came to him as he knelt before a slow-moving train filled with munitions destined for war. "As the front of the train pushed me backward and moved over me, the actual presence of Jesus flooded into my life." His spiritual experience during Christian social protest gives me a new understanding of the way God works with those who follow the Lord.

GOALS

An encompassing view of the gospel fuels this model of the visible church, which has five goals:

1. To provide a caring ministry to people who need to experience the caring fruits of Christ's presence in the world.
2. To provide a ministry opportunity for young people and adults which includes worship, study, fellowship, and service/proclamation.
3. To provide a ministry opportunity for young people through which they can also receive the spiritual gifts of those who are being served.

4. To relate the caring ministry experience to the whole congregation.
5. To relate the holistic ministry concern of the congregation to the broader community.

This model is drawn from many different specific programs of churches around the country. It involves nothing really new or unusual. The Care Corps embraces the principles of the visible church to form a critical mass of power to accomplish the goals.

A specific service project outside the immediate area should be targeted. Lists of work-camp locations are available from regional or national offices of most churches. However your pastor probably can give you the name of a classmate or friend who is serving in an area where a specific project of care could be developed. Or you may take some of your people to a program of an organization such as *Group* magazine. Those people have years of experience and can provide a practical model that will serve a local church well in the design of its own outreach.

Let's say your young people are suffering from a very ethnocentric view of life and the Christian faith. They have been overdosed by an inner directed experience in your local community. They can't imagine a community where there is suffering and great things to be discovered concerning the gospel. The concept of the church as a missionary society is absolutely alien to them.

You might pick Mexico or Haiti as your summer Care Corps site. You must make careful preparation and obtain some guidance. Contact someone who has had experience in work camps, or a consultant who actually has been in the foreign setting you have chosen. Accept a third-world option only if you have an experienced planner.

A church in Des Moines chose a small town in Mexico. Mission work was being conducted in that village by the church's denomination, so the local church had a solid connection from which to plan. The Mexican church designed the work to be done, and the complex arrangements to bring building supplies into Mexico were handled by experienced work-camp people.

Before the actual Care Corps experience, several things needed to be done. The people who would participate were recruited by the staff persons who worked with youth, and a number of programs were held with the young people, to which significant adults were invited. One meeting featured an amplified phone conversation with the missionaries in Mexico. Tough questions were raised by both the young people and the missionaries. "Why do you want to come?" "Are you motivated by compassion, guilt, or pity? Are these emotions the proper reasons for responding as Christians?"

These were hard challenges. The group studied Acts 9:10-19, among other passages. The passage in Acts tells the story of Paul's conversion and the encounter between the Apostle and Ananias, the Christian from Damascus. The youths were particularly struck by its message—that the interaction between those two people was one of interdependence. Paul was physically blind, but Ananias was spiritually blind because he couldn't see how God's grace could extend to someone like a criminal. In the act of Paul's healing, a mutual ministry was undertaken: They both were healed!

The implications of caring for others was suddenly expanded. Perhaps young people would receive from those they served! They quickly saw how the stance of anticipating potential blessing from others made their acts of care more acceptable to the recipients. Every young person had experienced being offered something by someone who condescended to them. The condescension made them as uncomfortable as their need to receive help. Many adults feel this way, and communicate it, in dealing with youth. "Your tears over a lost girlfriend is just puppy love, you will get over it."

The youths spent time working on verbal and nonverbal skills in communicating care. How do you flesh out the love of Christ when you can't speak the language? What are the little gestures which tell others they are important in the eyes of Jesus Christ? How do you confront living conditions that are so different from those in your modern suburban existence? How do you face a morning without a hair dryer or MTV?

While the students were working on practical tasks, theological foundations, and psychological preparation, the Care Corps began to work with the whole congregation. A flyer was prepared about the impending ministry, and representatives from different boards and segments of the church were invited to the weekly sessions of preparation. They were encouraged to participate in the struggle, and in the excitement that was emerging.

The members of the group wanted to develop ways they could share across cultural lines. How could they return hospitality with a hospitable gesture? They came up with songs, mime skits, art techniques, and other creative efforts, to be shared at the proper times.

There also developed several teams of "media messengers," who worked together to learn to use audio cassette recorders for interviewing and to capture the music and sounds of Mexico. They found this particularly useful for recording the Mexican church at worship. Other members of the team worked on taking slides. Consultants from a local radio station and newspaper came to help them learn more about interviewing, recording, and photography. This was particularly useful.

Some of the training sessions were held in a retreat setting. The impact of this preparation process did wonders for the youth programs. The leaders were very careful to include those who were not going to Mexico, and a prayer support group was formed for those youths.

Bake sales and other ordinary fund-raising projects were undertaken to raise money for the trip. Short Minute for Mission reports frequently were given during Sunday morning worship, and a prayer circle agreed to pray for the Care Corps regularly.

Months before their trip, a couple of young people went with an adult leader to the mass media and gave out a press release which detailed the total program. The media responded that they should be contacted later, closer to departure time. This response was expected, since the group only wanted the reporters and editors to be made aware of the program at that time.

A release was sent every other week after the visits; this increased to weekly several weeks before the visit. When the newspaper photographer consultant saw the quality of the teams' work, he suggested that they take black and white photos which "we might be able to use in the paper." Reporters agreed that the group could write an article about the trip upon their return.

Television contacts provided two appearances on talk shows. However, the Care Corps knew that the "news" side of the trip would be of most interest to television. Their departure and arrival would work well with this medium, and key young people were prepared to be spokespeople.

Only a few bumper stickers were printed, since they were expensive. They were given to people in the church who donated to the trip and those who understood the importance of witness to the broader community.

A teen computer hack who could not make the trip was able to glean all kinds of information about Mexico from billboards and other sources. He found people who had taken similar trips or knew people who had. And of course he sent out the news about their plans to other church and nonchurch computer folks.

It was interesting that the money for the trip came in so easily. While many people supported the usual activities, it was really the general interest of the whole church in the ministry outreach that caused contributions to come in.

The clergy and professional staff fully supported this ministry. Sermons were preached about mission concerns. The young people and adults were commissioned on the Sunday of their departure with a laying on of hands and not a few tears.

Television did cover the departure. (There are simply few good stories on Sunday.) The paper came through with an extensive story, and the radio station agreed to take a few phone reports from Mexico for their news programs.

The church was able to connect the phone line to the amplification system, and during the next two Sundays, live reports were taken by phone from members of the Care Corps! The pastor talked with the person on the phone and asked about the work and needs. Then the congregation prayed for their teams while they were still on the phone. It was a powerful moment. The church was deeply moved.

The second Sunday of their trip, the woman who was on the phone mentioned that they had become friends with a young boy with a club foot. She said the young people had decided that when they returned they would raise money to bring him to the United States for an operation. This sparked an immediate response from the congregation, and in just a few days the parishioners had found a doctor and hospital willing to help.

You can imagine what happened when the group returned. There was extensive media coverage and a great celebration at the church. When the young boy came a few weeks later, all the media connections came alive again.

I am pleased to report that the young boy had this operation, his foot has been fully restored, and he has returned to his village in Mexico. What an incredible ministry of care these young people unleashed!

AND SO . . .

While my account of this actual model has been expanded to include all the media touches, it is the experience of an actual church. The young boy who became part of their lives changed everyone who undertook the journey. The goals were accomplished beyond anyone's expectations. The program with the village has continued and is important in the life of this church.

This model beckons you. All your people with diverse interests have a common interest in doing something like this. The resources are also at hand. You simply need a unified vision of what you are seeking in terms of ministry. While the visible church demands a holistic approach, the dynamics are founded upon the same principles that guided the apostle Paul. He was limited to the use of a radically new mail system in the form of epistles, the accessibility of secular motifs and metaphors, and the availability of public reading and speaking. However, he pulled all the pieces together so that Jesus Christ might be known and experienced.

As you scan this model, don't stumble on small points of familiarity or strangeness in your potential participation as the visible church. The world is struggling to find the care of Christ. Your people, young and old, are poised to have their lives released in a way that will make a difference. The Care Corps offers an excellent starting point, by which many people will be blessed.

Chapter 16

PASSAGES: A MODEL
OF TESTIMONIES

"When you interviewed rock stars, you made the famous sound ordinary. Now you interview ordinary people, and you make them sound extraordinary." Kit Schooley was commenting about "Passages," the weekly radio program we had just begun. My pastoral-counselor friend is a shrewd observer of the way media forms relate to personal development. In fact, we have been communicating via audio cassete tape for the past fifteen years; we have discovered the sense of "foreshortened" history.

Kit would stop the tape and say that he was about to go into an important meeting, and in the next second I would hear his report, which actually had been recorded hours or days after the meeting. I didn't have to wait! I got all the news right there. I would notice, however, a different tone to his voice, and I could sense a change in attitude from the previous message.

Kit has utilized our discovery in counseling. People who face coping problems are given an audiocassette machine and told to record their feelings for a few minutes each day. They are not to play the tape back until their session. Then counselor and counselee listen to the tape and comment on the changes in the feelings. This enables the person being counseled to hear voice tones, emotional views, and perspectives over a whole week, and it is possible to gain a sense of emotional insight.

"Passages" is a weekly radio program which shares the stories of people who have faced incredible odds with hope and faith.

GOALS

There were five goals for this program of the visible church:

1. To provide a format in which stories of witness from Christians could be shared
2. To provide an exciting radio format which would encourage secular broadcasters to run the show free, as public affairs programming
3. To provide a training ground for Christians to learn how to produce national radio programming
4. To provide a media model which deemphasizes a single personality and lifts up ordinary people
5. To maximize the limited media budget of the regional church in media outreach.

I chose a twenty-eight-minute, thirty-second length for the show. I knew that our only hope to persuade stations to carry the program was to produce a show that would be stunning. It was also our conviction that ordinary Christians had extraordinary stories to tell.

The program needed a compelling and touching flow. We decided to open the show with a ten- or twenty-second "tease," a snatch of comment from the guest, something to capture the listeners' imagination, compassion, and need.

Interviews for the show come from many different places. In most cases, pastors simply suggest people they have met or worked with. Usually I interview them with an audio cassette recorder and a broadcast-quality microphone.

For example, I called a friend who had lost a teenage daughter two years before and asked if it was time to talk about it. She agreed. We met at her home and she talked for ninety minutes about the journey of pain and hope. At times, tears streamed down my face.

Anne Merrifield, a colleague, and I transferred the cassette to reel-to-reel tape. We then worked for about twenty hours with a razor blade and an edit block to cut out the parts of the tape we did not need.

A conversation is not a radio show. We must transform a face-to-face encounter into the restricted form of an audio experience. It was our conclusion that the audience would not listen to twenty-eight minutes of solid conversation. We edit the stories into sixty- to ninety-second segments with white spacer tape between them. We can look at the finished reel and see the breaks in the segments. It looks like the rings in a cut tree.

Three short identification statements at the beginning and a close at the end are literally taped onto the original reel.

We then spend several hours finding several songs with lyrics that lift up a particular segment of the interview. Special sound effects and general music beds also are chosen to provide a sound track for the story, much in the manner of a movie sound track.

One of our early shows particularly touched the hearts of our listeners. The program opened with the sound of wind blowing in a very haunting way. A woman's voice was heard: "The doctor told us my daughter had leukemia. She didn't have long to live."

The announcer added, "This is 'Passages,' the audio journal where people share their stories of hope and courage. Out guest today is Ruth Rylander, as she shares the story of her daughter." Bells now were heard over the wind. "Sometimes the road to death is slow and painful."

Ruth told the incredible story of her daughter's faith and courage. She shared the way her minister helped her when she told him she wished she were not a Christian—then she could be mad at God. "What makes you think you can't be angry at God? God can handle your anger," her minister answered. She told the listeners about the peace this insight gave her.

By the time she had talked about her faith and the church's help, she had established with the audience her right to make such statements. The reality and power of her story made the testimony powerful for both believer and nonbeliever.

Choosing the music for this show was difficult, but it is amazing that sometimes inspired choices are found. For instance, at one point Ruth described her promise to bring her daughter home so that she could die there: "I held her in my arms as she was dying. I tried to explain to her why we didn't make it. I think she understood." Next, Carol King heard singing, "I don't think I will make it home again."

The letters and calls in response to the program were tremendous. Other parents with similar situations wanted to talk with Ruth.

The show won the Gabriel Award from Unda, the Association

of Catholic Broadcasters, as the best locally produced radio program in the country. When I returned from Chicago with the award, I immediately went to visit Ruth and her husband, David. Ruth said she could see now that blessings were coming from her daughter's story. "Lynn had worried that her life had not made any difference. Maybe something is now emerging to indicate that her life was extremely important."

One of the most important things Ruth shared was that during the last days of Lynn's life, something important happened: "I suddenly realized that the whole world was dying. God was calling me to be a peacemaker."

As Ruth undertook this ministry, she met many negative responses from people in the defense industry. They didn't like her recitation of facts about the arms buildup. But when Ruth began to tell about how her daughter led her to be a peacemaker, there was a transformation in the audiences. They understood her motivation and stayed to hear her concern about peace in the world. She moved from grief to witness.

This is a model of the way media should be used in the visible church. Stories of sorrow can be transformed into testimonies of victory.

MEDIA

We started to distribute the show by writing to fifty stations. Dottie Ingram, secretary for the Presbyterian Media Mission, then called each station. Most turned us down, since each station that carried the show would be giving us free time worth $50 to $100 a week. This was serious business. The stations no loner need to run these kinds of public affairs programs. They certainly don't need to carry a show produced by Presbyterians, although the stories are told by people of all religious traditions and backgrounds.

We sent a demonstration tape to the stations. Fortunately, most program directors make decisions according to how well shows are produced, so our opening two minutes was very important. When they heard sound, music, and two voices, they knew there was a level of professionalism in the production of the show.

Soon stations started to make commitments, and we went on the air with twelve stations. At this writing the show is heard on 135 American stations, the NBC radio network, and The Armed Forces Overseas Network, receiving more than $700,000 worth of free time.

The show is now produced in two different lengths. A fourteen-minute, thirty-second version offered stations an option, and the number of stations increased by a third. More than three hundred fifty shows have been produced.

We also have released several series of spots utilizing the stories, one series hosted by Steve Allen, and we have won two additional Gabriel Awards, which aid greatly in the placement of our radio material. When stations know the material is judged best in the country, they find it easier to make the decision to air it. The awards also give our people something to be proud of. They deserve to be affirmed for their faithfulness to Jesus Christ.

At the end of each program we offer a free audio cassette of the show. We receive many responses and often receive calls from people with problems similar to those of the speaker.

The show is promoted heavily to the local churches across the area, and when the staff appears before the meeting of the regional churches, there often is a standing ovation. When the Gabriel Award was received, we actually passed the six-pound award to each person at the meeting. We wanted the people to handle it and realize that it was their witness to Christ that was being recognized.

One of the most important parts of obtaining public-affairs air time is servicing the stations. The computer is useful in collecting and utilizing data about particular stations in the areas served. The format, the kind of music, and the style of programming change quite regularly. Personnel also change continually. One program director who loves the show may be gone tomorrow, and the new person may not like your show.

The stations are called regularly with bits of news to remind the program directors how good the show is: "I just wanted to tell you we won a Wilbur Award for our show on South Africa. I'm going to send you some copy you might want to record for the show when it plays on your station. Of course, it gives the stations credit for the best show in the country last year."

In the process of editing, the show is shaped to fit the radio format. Yet we have been able to maintain an integrity in keeping with the original form.

The process of producing the show is one of the surprising features of this model. We have trained a corps of local folks from different walks of life to act as associate producers. Each person has been provided with a reel-to-reel machine. These people edit the interviews, aid in choosing the music, and assist me in mixing the show. The youngest producer was thirteen when he started. We have had unemployed workers, college students, communication school graduates, and a station program manager. The latter sought this role because he could not do this kind of creative work at his station.

I know of no other nationally syndicated, award-winning program that is actually produced by ordinary people.

There continue to be amazing moments on this extraordinary show. When the show featuring one man's story was broadcast, he was in a coma. His family, gathered around the bed, heard his testimony about the way Christ had led his life. It was a moving moment.

Many people say they have told us things that they never before have told anyone. Often these people will express a sense of relief that they have shared their story, and this will touch other people.

I remember standing at the door of a couple who had agreed to talk with me, but they now refused to open the door. "I don't think we have anything to say." I had to talk for several minutes to convince them to let me interview them. Of course, their story of caring for older people was wonderful.

Mass media tend to make ordinary people feel that they have nothing to offer. But the more we look up to stars, the more we look down on ourselves.

The visible church utilizes mass media in such a way that it lifts up the people of God. In the hands of those who embrace this concept, the media are merely means of serving the gospel that has come to us. The host of witnesses to Christ deserve the opportunity to reach others.

And So . . .

This broadcast model demonstrates that the visible church can touch the lives of thousands by utilizing our greatest asset, our people and their lives in Christ. The secular media world will work with us in a symbiotic manner. Their needs and ours are not really in conflict. They want to hold as many listeners as possible, make a profit, and keep their Federal Communication Commission license. We can help them with the first and last needs. We provide extension promotion among the churches of the stations that carry our shows.

You may know nothing about radio, but there are folks in your area who do. The leader of the visible church needs to be a person who can draw upon the resources in the community. You do have the reservoir of amazing stories for which mass media so yearns. The biggest problem that faces the creators of media is the lack of stories to tell.

Look into radio as a way to reach out to others. It offers an amazing way to touch the lives of others in a special way. It is also one of the best mediums for getting the most for your money.

Chapter 17

LET YOUR FINGERS DO THE TALKING: A MODEL FOR THE VISIBLE EAR

The sales manager of the car dealership stopped pacing. He swung around and stared at us. Eddie's frightening gaze scanned each of the ten salesmen in the conference room.

For the past hour, he had been trying to stir us to a new level of blazing sales desire. His performance mixed cliches of inspiration, fear, and greed. He must have drawn upon every B-movie locker-room scene he had ever seen for his material. Our leader was now ready to present his new sales plan. His bloodshot eyes seemed to direct their gaze at me.

"You are standing on the brink of amazing income. Bonuses, prizes, and glory await each of you. You will carry this dealership to new sales heights. We will beat our quota and surpass our competition. My plan is based on a very simple approach. It can't . . . it won't fail. I want each of you to make fifty phone calls each day."

Eddie paused for impact. The salesmen shivered. Calling fifty cold prospects each day was the last thing in the world we wanted to do. What madness! This guy must be nuts.

"To make sure this plan works, I want a daily log of each call you make. Write your comments on each card with the phone number after you make your call. This will be done each day, for each car. No telephone calls, no draw!"

We winced at the prospect of trying to sell a car over the phone. Who ever sold a car over the phone? Who ever bought a car over the phone? However, if we were to receive our basic salary, we would have to return fifty cards daily, with notations on each contact.

"How many cards," we wondered silently, "could we dare to return with the notation, 'no answer'?"

On the third day, I stumbled upon my most feared situation. The phone had rung the required eight times, and I was about to hang up with a sense of relief. Suddenly the sound of a panting, aged voice could be heard: "Yes, yes, yes?"

I had just identified myself as calling from the car dealership when the man screamed at me, "What? What? How dare you call me! My wife is in intensive care. I had to run up a flight of stairs from the basement to answer this phone, and I have a serious heart condition. Young man, what kind of morals do you have?"

In spite of that unnerving personal experience more than thirty years ago, I have revised my opinion of the persuasive role our phone systems can play. It is true that some questionable things still take place. People do buy diamonds, purchase gold-mining stock, seek pornographic conversations, and go on "talking dates" with anonymous strangers. Phone hucksters are relentless in their pursuit of our dollars. More capable salespeople apparently succeed where my fellow car-sales folks in Detroit failed so long ago.

On the other hand, the telephone also assists in life-giving tasks. It can deliver emergency health treatment, reach out to touch loved ones over long distance, seek funds for good causes, or locate a desperately needed human organ for a transplant.

For the past twenty years, I have hosted radio talk-shows and utilized the phone. Yes, the telephone can also be a means of ministry. Thousands of people have called me with stories of personal trial and victory. Moments that involved drugs, AIDS, unemployment, divorce, abuse, sacrifice, love, and hope have been revealed and shared through the phone. Frustration, fear, anger, despair, and humor have emerged through this combination of phone and radio. People have felt the love of Jesus Christ through this common instrument of communication. The phone can be used for both good and evil. It can be both a blessing and a curse.

TELEMARKETING

Local congregations are now discovering the telephone as a special way to communicate with the community. In fact, telemarketing is now one of the hottest outreach methods. The traditional practice of selling over the phone (via human and computer) has been refashioned into an exciting new opportunity for ministry and pre-evangelism.

For example, a church in suburban Philadelphia called seventeen thousand people—half the phone book—during a short span of time. They set this energetic outreach in a holistic context. They trained callers and developed a script which enabled their folks to reach out with sensitivity and care. They let the persons who answered the phone know who was calling and quickly asked whether they presently had a church home. If the persons declared an affiliation, they wished them well and passed on to the next call.

The church also developed a special hospitality Sunday for visitors. A user-friendly bulletin which could be understood by strangers, a set of special greeters, and a meal—all were prepared especially for the guests. Two hundred seventy new people came as a result of calling program! The new members' class, which started the week after visitors' Sunday, boasted the biggest attendance in its history. They are now preparing to call the other half of their phone directory.

Another church in Pennsylvania utilized this method as the basis for founding a new congregation. The team that developed the church called everyone in the community to seek opinions on what kinds of ministry were needed by the people. A terse series of questions was developed to aid the process.

The Benefits

As a result of this telephone survey, or telemarketing outreach, this new-church-development project accomplished three goals.

In the first place, it raised awareness about the new church in the community. The phone calls were followed by mailers to each household, which made a second impression on those who received the communication.

In the second place, the group was able to identify perceived needs of the people to be served. The points of entry into the lives of the people to be touched by the gospel were found. This is a vital step for the visible church. To whom are we presenting

Christ? What aspect of salvation history will reach them most deeply?

Third, the developers were able to formulate a specific ministry plan. In a matter of weeks they came back to the community with a strong series of church programs based on results of their calls. This gave the new church a solid foundation of bonding between the community and the gospel. A sense of "in response to your request" could be used in announcing the programs.

New Patterns

A church in Bakersfield, California, utilized telemarketing to touch the lives of people in their community. They used a phone directory keyed to streets. And they reached some interesting insights.

For instance, when they found that one or two families were very turned off by the church, just about everyone else on that street would have the same attitude! This information was used to skip such enclaves of hostility.

Other churches might have decided to act differently on this information. A special approach might have been developed for these pockets of resistance. This kind of information could not be discovered without actually talking to the people we are seeking to reach.

The Price to Be Paid

It is clear that this aural visibility offers an exciting option for any congregation that takes outreach seriously. But there is a price to be paid for this kind of undertaking—congregational support is vital to the execution of such a labor-intensive model. Telemarketing requires a solid staff of well-trained callers to make the quick, intensive impact. This means of outreach demands a blanketing effect to stir a reaction in the community.

Training can be developed by using the local phone company's resources. These folks have literature, and even personnel to help design your specific program. Your national and regional denominational offices of evangelism also will be able to provide some case studies. They may even have names of contact people who have utilized the phone in this manner. Call other churches that have used this method of reaching out to the community. They will be glad to share what they have learned.

Helping others experience the hospitality of Christ is a major motif of this book, and this concern demands that some specific preparations be developed for a new person being caught in this net of concern. Guests may be attracted by the promise that their spiritual needs can be met by your faith community. However, the fact that they are not currently participants in the life of your congregation may suggest that they suspect (correctly) that they cannot find what they need in your current programming.

The presence of each new person changes the specific nature of the community of Christ through his or her needs and gifts. You can fill the church on a particular Sunday by utilizing telemarketing and other clues in this book. However, will the strangers come again, after they have experienced the way you express the gospel through your congregation? Will visitors encounter the incarnation of God's love through your visible community? Will they intimately perceive that the gospel is for them, at this moment, in this place, with these people?

Churches that utilize the phone successfully not only have shaped an invitational event for visitors, but have gone even further. In the phone encounters, they have actually listened to the subtle cries of need from persons seeking Jesus Christ. Their ears have become attuned to the sounds of those for whom Christ has come. The most authentic use of telemarketing by Christians draws upon both a programming and a spiritual sensitivity in their responses to those cries of need.

New programs, different educational opportunities, changes in liturgical patterns, new child-care programs, and other special preparations must be provided for the guest in our midst. One church followed its telemarketing campaign with alterations in the parking lot. It posted signs that reserved choice parking spaces near the doors for guests!

Follow-up is also a key factor in making the phone connection work. Just judging the guest to be present for worship on a given Sunday does not complete the evangelism task. How will the babe in Christ be challenged to stretch, to grow, to change spiritually? Faithful, relentless pursuit by the people of God in caring for the stranger—this is at the bottom of all good telemarketing approaches.

YES, BUT . . .

In some cases, your governing board or individuals in the
congregation initially may react negatively to such a model of
outreach. These voices of dissent may suggest that using
telemarketing for Christian outreach is being too much like the
commercial forces in the world. It is important to hear what such
resistance may be revealing.

We have often talked in this book about how our forebears in
the faith were enabled by God to transform secular communication forms into moments of grace. Secular phrases, Stoic poems,
pagan theological terms, and the most popular communication
techniques were transformed to glorify God before others.

Indeed, some will resist the opportunity to let their fingers do
the walking because they don't discern the connection between
their theology and this kind of evangelism. Yet, there may also be
resistance that springs from a fear that the newcomers will bring
change. They correctly suspect that the energy required to
incarnate the hospitality of Christ may endanger their self-
interest. Loving the stranger in the name of Christ forces the
congregational focus to shift from serving only the home folks and
their personal quest for salvation. Of course, each person's
spiritual search is vital. Yet Christ calls us to lay down our lives
for others. This means we should desert our own comfort and
self-interest.

However, there are special blessings for those who surrender
their personal needs to the ministry of service to others. The
stranger is to be embraced not only for his or her sake, but in
order to claim our own authenticity. The guest is the bearer of
the gospel for us also. The host at the feast that is called in the
name of Christ is always blessed by the strangers invited to the
table. We receive from God only as we share God with others.

The telephone can be a real blessing in the hands of believers
called to be the visible church. What kind of renewal could take
place in a parish whose members are committed to hospitality
and dedicated to calling fifty people each week? The hands of
believers, directed by the finger of God, will be the media of
outreach for the kingdom of God.

Chapter 18

A SUMMING UP:
IF IT FITS . . .

The fifteen-year-old high school student twitched nervously on the low stool. He had brought out more than forty boxes of shoes for the customer. Down to a final choice, the woman slowly pivoted before the mirror. "I don't know." The black patent pumps sparkled in the light. "What do you think?"

The young shoe salesman knelt before the woman. He carefully felt along the heel, arch, and toe. "How does it fit?"

It is strange that this same question comes back to me as I survey this romp through the concept of the visible church. I think about you, the reader. Has there been an emotional, rational, practical, and spiritual bonding between the message sent to you from other folks in ministry? Does the swirl of ideas and dreams seem close to the edge of your needs and visions? How does this demanding and exciting concept of making the gospel of Jesus Christ visible to the community through your church fit with who you are?

Those comfortably shod with the perspective of the visible church tend to judge the fit through ten points of contact.

HOW DOES IT FIT? The leader in the visible church is transformed by his or her relationship to Jesus Christ. At a time when many leaders are uncomfortable with admitting such a relationship in public, this attribute is vital.

This seems an obvious measurement of leadership in the church. Yet some extreme folk of faith have claimed a public affirmation of Jesus Christ which includes attributes of behavior that are embarrassing for other Christians. In response, modest folks unfortunately have given up articulation of faith.

Jesus Christ is the only anchor that can protect those who venture into the secular environment as the visible church. There are many seductive moments in the process of utilizing electronic media. We have seen the public countryside littered with the wrecks of authenticity and reputation of those who became lost in their success. The most successful participation in modern media brings us so close to the forms of communication that the content can easily be changed.

Jesus Christ is the love and grace of God become flesh. He is the medium and message of God for us. It is this embrace of God and our continuous responding hug that keeps us faithful to our calling.

The means of grace are vital to those who will lead others. The leader of the visible church can fit into this awesome role only through prayer, Bible study, receiving the sacraments, and belonging to the communion of saints.

HOW DOES IT FIT? The leader in the visible church acknowledges that he or she is a creative person. Again, the obvious attribute for leadership often is denied by current leaders: "I'm not a creative person." This denial is based on an elitist view of creativity. Because I can't sing, dance, play an instrument, draw, or write poetry, I was told through all my formative years that I was not creative. Also we are surrounded by people who are recognized for creativity because of their clothing, speech, or reputation.

I contend that creativity is the gift from God which enables us to create wholeness in the midst of fragmentation. God provides the supreme model by which chaos was transformed into order. If a person is in Jesus Christ, the old has passed away and the new has come. It is the new, which has been transformed from the old, that represents creativity.

All the probes, dreams, and plans offered in this book have resulted from resources that already exist in every local church situation. It is the leader for the visible church who will provide the vision to bring those pieces together to take Jesus Christ to the world.

Creativity, as a gift from God, assumes that it is the work of the Holy Spirit which makes possible the transformation of the parts into an authentic totality. The creative leader is not drawing only upon his or her resources. There is a sense that the whole historical community of faith is an inspiration or guide into this confusing and demanding media-oriented age.

The creativity possessed by the leader is not a possession to be hoarded. Since all the resources and ideas issue from the community, all the contributions made to that which the leader receives must be shared with others.

HOW DOES IT FIT? The leader for the visible church is an enabler. This person may or may not be a member of the clergy, but he or she is extremely important to what will or will not happen. It takes at least one person to catch the inspiration of the Holy Spirit concerning what God will do through a particular congregation in order for this concept of outreach to work.

This approach to leadership does not have many models. In just about every activity, we desire strong, single-minded leadership. Give us the coach, business executive, or military person who tells everyone what to do, and the community is satisfied. Whether such leadership is really as successful as it might be is never challenged.

Also, our leadership image is confused because of a distant leadership situation in reality. In other words, many times when people are placed in top positions, they carry the title and are given distracting duties, but the real power is elsewhere. This mode seems to support the traditional leadership model, while a different style is actually in operation. The church is particularly guilty of this in its tradition of pampered pastors: Keep them busy with trivial things while the real decisions (financial) are made in a small circle of power people. This is an overstatement of the case in most situations, but it does describe the tendency to fall into a leadership model that will fail to make the visible church possible.

The enabling leadership style releases creativity and power in others. This kind of person helps others excel in the gifts of ministry. But it is easier to espouse this attribute than to live it. When I see a student reaching further than I have indicated, and I realize that she will accomplish more than I have, I have a moment of doubt. Will I be needed if she has gone beyond me? However, there is no other way leadership can function in the age of the visible church. We can be thankful that God enables us to feel our worth and value beyond our ability to prove ourselves.

The enabling leadership mode is rooted in knowing whose we are. We belong to Christ. We live, breathe, act, and thrive because of Christ. We have been chosen—for no objective reason—but simply because God loves us and redeems us. No one can threaten the security of this relationship. So when another person responds to our leadership and exceeds our experience, we can smile and be thankful that we have helped a person on the journey of service.

HOW DOES IT FIT? The leader for the visible church is curious. Curiosity killed a cat, and certainly is dangerous when people find something they had not expected.

Leonard Nimoy, of *Star Trek* and Shakespeare fame, told me about a conversation he had years ago when he was in college. He was driving a cab in Los Angeles, and one evening he picked up a fare at a downtown hotel. He recognized the Congressman from his home state.

When the Congressman learned that Leonard was from his district, he spent the next fifty minutes grilling him about his personal views, his observations about fares, and his dreams for the future. Leonard was impressed by John F. Kennedy's curiosity about all of life.

It is dangerous to listen and inquire about that which we don't know. I am always amazed by the censorious looks I receive from friends when they learn that I have toured with a major rock star, been an extra in a Hollywood movie, interviewed people on skid row, or ordered a six-foot Godzilla.

I have recently experienced the inability of others to discern important clues to ministry in unexpected places. If Moses had not been curious and stopped to see why the bush was burning, he probably would not have heard God calling. This age has many burning bushes. God is initiating probes into our ministry in many unexpected ways. The leadership for the visible church is curious.

HOW DOES IT FIT? The leader for the visible church is a risk-taker. "When you were fired, I almost stood up and defended you." Waves of feelings came across me as I heard this statement from the stranger in front of me. A decade had passed.

I was no longer without a job, friends, and resources. Now I was the keynote speaker at a huge educational gathering. It was safe to talk with me.

Risking is never easy. It runs against our need of creature comforts. Who would place themselves in the way of resistance and struggle? Just about everyone who develops and accomplishes things does just that—no pain, no gain.

Yet our institutional training within and outside the church encourages a survivalist attitude: Don't go out on a limb. Every wise person seems to counsel the cautious route. I find that it is no easier to risk today, after twenty years of pushing to the edge, than it was the first time.

I believe that risk for the Christian is based on the biblical model. Jesus calls us to face the wind of culture and self-interest and be the persons he has called us to be. The world will most likely treat us the way he was treated, but we are promised that the risktaker will be comforted in times of trial.

To be a servant of Jesus Christ in our times is to risk. The world is simply not Christian. To be radically obedient to Jesus Christ is to be put in jeopardy. To make visible the body of Christ in such a way that others will know him is to live dangerously.

HOW DOES IT FIT? The leader for the visible church is an inclusive person. Again, the traditional pattern of the church is to draw a circle and spend time measuring and focusing on the space within it. Yet when we draw a circle on the ground, we have divided the whole universe. Why not explore the area outside the lines?

The Incarnation has not divided the world into neat spacial dominions of safe and unsafe realms. The event of Jesus Christ permits us to go into unknown places with unknown people, in order to find the realms of God's grace. It is the embrace that transforms the stranger and the alien into a kinship.

Such a leadership perspective not only provides new resources and options, but it enables the church to find new pockets of people who need Christ. The tight racial, social, and theological boundaries of contemporary Christian communities is a scandal to the faith. Programs for church development, with their calls for homogeneous evangelism, tend to nurture such divisions. There is no such elitist attitude in an encounter with the biblical witness. When Christ found me, or I found Christ, my ethnocentric views on class and race were turned upside down. I was ushered into a kinship forged through the blood of Jesus Christ.

This also is a dangerous attitude. People will judge you for putting on these shackles of faith. You will look at that which is dirty, abusive, and objectionable and see signs of grace. You will work with resources and forces judged negatively by the world. You will find colleagues and consultants in the secular world and help them serve the gospel. Others in the faith community will abuse leaders who demonstrate these qualities.

HOW DOES IT FIT? The leaders for the visible church are restless. They will be critical about what is and what has been. The historical church will be seen as one that has sold itself to cultural forces and anti-Christian attitudes, but it will remain their parent. The restlessness of this kind of leadership causes a kind of lover's quarrel. Yet, there always will be a clear recognition that there is no life without the church.

The restless spirit is one without a final resting place or lasting comfort. The work and accomplishment of yesterday will not be enough. The moment of standing before the crowd to accept the award will be strangely unsatisfying. The campaign successfully completed will be inadequate to quiet the fire burning within for more work.

Leadership with this kind of longing is not driven for success or accomplishment. It is the beckoning of Christ for faithfulness that keeps the leaders going. The sensitivity to the needs of the world and the power of the gospel make complacency impossible.

This premise also suggests that leadership for the visible church is aware of its capacity for change and growth. It is restless to break the bonds of past performance. Most people want to stand on what they have gained in the past. Like Peter and the disciples, they want to stay on the mount and bask in the illumination of Jesus and the prophets during the moment of transfiguration. However, Jesus does not permit this luxury. They must restlessly move on to undertake the ministry that lies ahead.

Restlessness will always put you in conflict with those who long to live the same moment again and again. For them, continuity can be achieved only in the frozen frame from the past. But for the restless person of faith in the visible church, Jesus Christ is the stream of reality that links past, present, and future.

HOW DOES IT FIT? The leaders for the visible church are persons who feel that their lives make a difference. This is not an outlook held by the usual winner.

The models for leadership move in an anticipation of hope. These folks have an optimistic outlook. They are possibility thinkers. Their sense of hope is biblically rooted. The God of creation, revealed in Jesus Christ, will empower. Their hopefulness is based on this kind of reality. It may mean that their efforts undertaken on behalf of the visible church will not succeed, yet the leaders know that their lives will make a difference.

It is easy to become mired in hopelessness. I meet so many fantastic people who perceive that they are helpless. "I am over forty-five and churches really don't want me."

"I am a woman and the church won't recognize my contribution to ministry."

The winner in the visible church is the person who can engender confidence and hope in others. This is a special gift that is vital to the visible church. I remember moments in the midst of a media project when time was running out, equipment wasn't working, and everyone was exhausted. "Let's get going. It's going to be fantastic. We will do it once again." I believe what I am saying, but I also must deal with a sense of doubt. Yet it is my role to look for hope in my leadership of others.

Having crossed the half-century mark, I find something strange taking over my life. I now believe that anything I can dream, I can make reality—if I will pay the price. This weird confidence is both a burden and a blessing. If you understand creative visions as being a gift of God, and if you believe you have the power to transform dreams into reality, you are responsible! If you don't follow your vision, you have doomed a divine gift.

HOW DOES IT FIT? Leadership for the visible church is self-critical. We are not schooled to be really sensitive to our own failings. It is true that guilt and simple piety often value a self-effacing stance before others, but that is not the self-critical view we are defining here.

Christian self-analysis liberates. When a centipede was asked which of its hundred legs it moved first, it thought and thought about the question, but could not decide. And through indecision, it found itself unable to move at all.

Criticism can work the same way. I remember a teacher who made a public comment about my singing. The class thought her frog analogy was very funny. But I have not sung in public since that sixth-grade class.

Christian enablers of the visible church are rooted in their calling in Christ. God must be the final judge. The standard of appraisal is set by that relationship. We can judge ourselves honestly and harshly without becoming disabled or discouraged.

"I have never met a person as confident as you." My friend was sharing what he thought of me. Yet no one is more critical of my work than I am. I know how far I fall short of serving Christ. I have been given so many visions, so many opportunities, and yet I am weak. I do not carry out each part as well as I must.

Most leaders in the church of our day live without helpful criticism. It is true that enemies complain and friends affirm, but this is not the kind of criticism that helps a person grow and become effective. One needs to be one's own most severe critic. There is no place in the visible church for self-deception. Christ gives us a clear eye and firm confidence so that we can become better.

HOW DOES IT FIT? Last, leadership in the visible church embraces forgiveness. The source of this divine gift is God. We are forgiven of all sins through the work of Christ. This act of grace is unearned, undeserved, and unending.

The kind of ministry called forth by this book will bring much heartache and failure. Yet, your self-criticism and honesty can never undercut your call or your hope. You are always forgiven in order to serve boldly again.

And because we are forgiven, we can forgive others—the many people who will sin against you and your risks on behalf of the gospel.

This point of contact has been particularly hard for me. During my twenty years of free-lance ministry, I have been ill-treated by